Contents

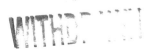

Map of the book

SPEAKING	WRITING	GRAMMAR	VOCABULARY
How are/were computers used in your school?	*Specific computer applications*	*Present simple passive* Data + *3rd person singular verb*	*Word fields: computers in education, banks, sports, airports, medicine, factories, entertainment*
			Basic terminology: hardware, software, peripherals, input/output devices, central processing unit
Your ideal computer system		*Contextual reference* *Defining relative clauses*	*Acronyms and abbreviations:* CPU, ALU, RAM, ROM, bit, SIMMs
	Translations		*Prefixes:* deci-, hexadeci-, kilo-, mega-, giga-, mini-, micro-, bi-, tri-, mono-, multi-
Role play: buying a computer	*Recommending a computer to a friend*		*Vocabulary tree: terminology*
Describing and identifying input devices	*Describing a joystick*	*for* + -ing which + *verb* which/that is used + to + *inf.*	*Word field: input devices* *Symbols and special keys* *Mouse actions:* click, drag
		Comparatives and superlatives	*Word building: suffixes* *Persuasive words in advertisements*
Describing your computer screen	*Explaining tables*	*Instructions and advice: imperative,* should, ought to	*Monitors:* resolution, pixels, display, hertz, VGA, LCD, CRT, phosphors
Describing the printer you would like to use	*The pros and cons of the printer you use*	*Discourse cohesion: reference signals and linking devices* *Comparison: revision*	*Types of printers:* dot-matrix, ink-jet, thermal and laser printers, photosetters, plotters
Discussing devices for computer users with vision and mobility limitations	*A letter asking for information about I/O equipment for disabled workers*	*Noun phrases; modifiers*	Braille, speech synthesizers, Morse code, optical head pointer, voice recognition, screen-pointing device
How to protect your disks		*Instructions with* must/must not	Floppies: track, sector, format, magnetic, read/write heads, directory, DD/HD *Suffixes:* -ic, -ism, -ize, -izable, -er
	Completing a hard disk advertisement		*Hard disks:* access time, data transfer rate, password, fragmentation, removable cartridge
Choosing the most suitable storage devices for specific purposes	*Completing a table with relevant information about optical disks*	*Discourse cohesion: reference signals and connectors and modifiers*	*Acronyms and abbreviations:* laser, ms, CD-ROM, CD-R, DVD-ROM

Thanks

The author would especially like to express his gratitude to Paz, Marina and Violeta.
My special thanks to Will Capel for his help.
Thanks are also due to teachers and students of Instituto Pilar Lorengar, Zaragoza.
Angel Benedí for his generous advice on technical aspects.
James Dale for editing the typescript.

Acknowledgements

The author and publishers are grateful to the authors, publishers and others who have given permission for the use of copyright material identified in the text. It has not been possible to identify the sources of all the material used and in such cases the publishers would welcome information from copyright owners.

(p = page; t = top; c = centre; b = bottom; l = left; r = right)

p. 31: Reprinted from *Your First Computer* by Alan Simpson, by permission of SYBEX Inc. ISBN 0-89588-752-5, Copyright 1992, SYBEX Inc. All rights reserved; pp. 46–47: Adapted extract from 'Computers for the disabled' by Joseph J. Lazzaro, reprinted with permission from the June 1993 issue of *BYTE* magazine © by McGraw-Hill Inc. New York NY. All rights reserved; pp. 74, 77, 98–99: Reprinted from *Understanding Computers* by Nathan Shedroff,
J. Sterling Hutto, and Ken Fromm, by permission of SYBEX Inc. ISBN 0-7821-1284-X, Copyright 1993, SYBEX Inc. All rights reserved; p. 97: Extract from *Introduction to Computer Graphics* by permission of Hewlett-Packard Limited; pp. 103–104: Permission granted from the article 'Upgrading to Multimedia', *PC Upgrade*, June 1993 issue, a publication of Bedford Communications, Inc., New York, New York.

p 2 tl The Stock Market/A. Skelley; p 2 tr Tony Stone Images/Walter Hodges; p 2 bl Peter Menzel/Science Photo Library; p 2 br Sporting Pictures (UK) Limited; p 5 Pictor International; pp 12, 23 l, 24 l, 67 c Compaq Computers Limited; p 15 Taheshi Takahara/Science Photo Library; p 21 tr PC World; pp 21, bl, br, 24 r, 66 b, 69 Reproduced by kind permission of Apple Computer UK Limited; pp 23 r, 42 Hewlett-Packard Limited; p 35 Epson (UK) Limited; p 45 tl Sally Lancaster/ Format Photographers; p 4 tr Richard T. Nowitz/Science Photo Library; p 45 bl Action for Disability, Newcastle-upon-Tyne/Simon Fraser/Science Photo Library; p 45 br De Repentigny, Publiphoto Diffusion/Science Photo Library; p 46 l Peter Menzel/Science Photo Library; p 46 r Sally Lancaster/ Format Photographers; p 47 AbilityNet; p 51 PowerStock/Zefa; pp 55, 60, 67 t IBM (UK) Limited; p 59 b The Stock Market/Jean Miele; p 62 Greg Evans International; pp 66 t, 66 c, 102, 113 Box shots reprinted with permission from Microsoft Corporation; pp 67 b, 112 Sun Microsystems Incorporated; pp 71, 73, 76, 77 t, c, b, 79, 81 b, 87 Screen shots reprinted by permission from Microsoft Corporation; pp 88, 90 Netscape Communications Corporation; p 91 Eudora Qualcomm Incorporated; p 98 Screen Shot of Adobe® Pagemaker® reproduced with the permission of Adobe Systems Europe Limited; p 120 Telegraph Colour Library/V.C.L./Nick Clements; p 122 John Walmsley Photo-Library; p 124 PowerStock/Zefa/Index; p 125 John Birdsall Photography; p 126 l Kind permission of British Telecommunications PLC; p 126 r Screen from Teletext on ITV and Channel Four, by permission of Teletext Limited; p 128 Tony Stone Images/Andrew Errington; p 138 tl Photo of Mobile Access 120 phone provided as a courtesy by the Personal Mobile Communications Division, Mitsubishi Wireless Communication Incorporated; p 138 tr NASA/Science Photo Library; p 138 bl Tony Stone Images/ Dan Bosler; p 138 br WorldGate Incorporated; p 140 Photo courtesy of Philips Electronics; p 141 Psion Computers PLC; p 142 Cartoon by Patrick Blower. Photographs on pp 7, 59, 66, 102, 103, 113, 136, by Nigel Luckhurst.

Picture research by Sandie Huskinson-Rolfe of PHOTOSEEKERS.

Computers today

Learning objectives

In this section you will learn how to:

- talk and write about computer applications in everyday life
- recognize the basic components of a computer system and understand their functions
- understand the structure of different CPUs (central processing units)
- understand the units of memory (bits, bytes, KB, MB, GB)
- build up new words by using prefixes
- buy a computer from a shop
- use synonyms, acronyms and abbreviations when talking about computers.

Unit 1 *Computer applications*

1 Match the pictures

A **Computers have many applications in a great variety of fields. Look at these photographs of different situations and match them with texts 1 to 4 below.**

a

b

c

d

1 Computers can help students perform mathematical operations and solve difficult questions. They can be used to teach courses such as computer-aided design, language learning, programming, mathematics, etc.

  PCs (personal computers) are also used for administrative purposes: for example, schools use databases and word processors to keep records of students, teachers and materials.

2 Race organizers and journalists rely on computers to provide them with the current positions of riders and teams in both the particular stages of the race and in the overall competition.

Workstations in the race buses provide the timing system and give up-to-the-minute timing information to TV stations. In the press room several PCs give real-time information on the state of the race. Computer databases are also used in the drug-detecting tests for competitors.

3 Computers store information about the amount of money held by each client and enable staff to access large databases and to carry out financial transactions at high speed. They also control the automatic cash dispensers which, by the use of a personal coded card, dispense money to clients.

4 Airline pilots use computers to help them control the plane. For example, monitors display data about fuel consumption and weather conditions.

In airport control towers, computers are used to manage radar systems and regulate air traffic.

On the ground, airlines are connected to travel agencies by computer. Travel agents use computers to find out about the availability of flights, prices, times, stopovers and many other details.

B **Match these captions with the pictures.**

Using an automatic cash dispenser ☐

In education, computers can make all the difference ☐

Organizing the Tour de France demands the use of computer technology ☐

Controlling air traffic ☐

C **When you read texts like these, you don't always need to understand every word. But there are words which you can guess from the context. Look at these words. Are they nouns (n), verbs (v) or adjectives (adj)?**

1 workstation ..... 2 data ..... 3 perform ..... 4 automatic ..... 5 monitor .....
6 financial ..... 7 store ..... 8 connected ..... 9 word processor ..... 10 large .....

Now find the words in texts 1 to 4, and match them with the meanings below.

a information ☐ g self-acting, mechanical ☐
b execute (do) ☐ h screen ☐
c connected with money ☐ i powerful computer usually
d keep (save) ☐ connected to a network ☐
e massive ☐ j program used for text manipulation ☐
f linked ☐

D **Look at text 1 again and discuss these questions.**

1 How are/were computers used in your school?
2 What other areas of study would benefit from the introduction of computers?

2 Listening

▱◉ **Listen to these people talking about how they use computers at work and write each speaker's job in the table.**

electrical engineer   secretary   librarian   composer

Speaker	Job	What they use computers for
1		
2		
3		
4		

Now listen again and write what each speaker uses their computer for.

3 Reading

A **Write a list of as many uses of the computer, or computer applications, as you can think of.**

B **Now read the text below and underline any applications that are not in your list.**

What can computers do?

Computers and microchips have become part of our everyday lives: we visit shops and offices which have been designed with the help of computers, we read magazines which have been
5   produced on computer, we pay bills prepared by computers. Just picking up a telephone and dialling a number involves the use of a sophisticated computer system, as does making a flight reservation or bank transaction.

10   We encounter daily many computers that spring to life the instant they're switched on (e.g. calculators, the car's electronic ignition, the timer in the microwave, or the programmer inside the TV set), all of which use chip
15   technology.

What makes your computer such a miraculous device? Each time you turn it on, it is a tabula rasa that, with appropriate hardware and software, is capable of doing anything you ask. It is a calculating machine that speeds up financial   20 calculations. It is an electronic filing cabinet which manages large collections of data such as customers' lists, accounts, or inventories. It is a magical typewriter that allows you to type and print any kind of document — letters, memos or   25 legal documents. It is a personal communicator that enables you to interact with other computers and with people around the world. If you like gadgets and electronic entertainment, you can even use your PC to relax with computer games.   30

4 Language work: The present simple passive

Look at the HELP box and then read the sentences.
Fill in the blanks with the correct form of the verbs in brackets.

Example

Houses (design) .... with the help of computers.
Houses are designed with the help of computers.

1 Various terminals (connect) ....
   to this workstation.

2 Microcomputers (know) .... as 'PCs'.

3 Magazines (typeset) .... by computers.

4 When a particular program is run, the data (process)
   .... by the computer very rapidly.

5 Hard disks (use) .... for the
   permanent storage of information.

6 The drug-detecting test in the Tour de France (support)
   .... by computers.

7 All the activities of the computer system (coordinate)
   .... by the central processing unit.

8 In some modern systems information (hold) .... in optical disks.

> **HELP box**
> **The present simple passive**
>
> - You form the present simple passive
>   with *am/is/are* + past participle, e.g.:
>   - *This program **is written** in a special
>   computer language.*
>   - *Programs and data **are** usually
>   **stored** on disks.*
>
> - Remember that the word *data* takes
>   a singular verb (3rd person singular)
>   when it refers to the information
>   operated on in a computer program.
>   - *The data **is** ready for processing.*

*Computers have
revolutionized the
design process*

5 Other applications

A   **In small groups, choose one of the areas in the diagram below and discuss what computers can do in this area.**

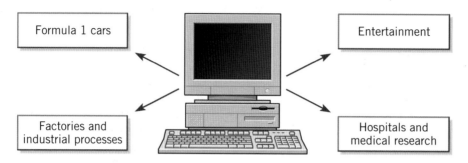

Formula 1 cars

Entertainment

Factories and industrial processes

Hospitals and medical research

Useful words

Formula 1: *racing car, car body, design, mechanical parts, electronic components, engine speed*

Entertainment: *game, music, animated image, multimedia, encyclopedia*

Factories: *machinery, robot, production line, computer-aided manufacturing software*

Hospitals: *patients, medical personnel, database program, records, scanner, diagnose, disease, robot, surgery*

Useful constructions

Computers are used to ...

A PC can also be used for ...

Computers can help ... make ... control ... store ... keep ... provide ... manage ... give ... perform ... measure ... test ... provide access to ...

B   **Now write a short paragraph summarizing your discussion. Then ask one person from your group to give a summary of the group's ideas to the rest of the class.**

Examples

In business, computers are used for financial planning, accounting and specific calculations.

In the office, computers are used to write letters and keep records of clients, suppliers and employees.

Unit 2 *Configuration*

1 Warm-up

In pairs, label the elements of this computer system. Then read the text in Task 2 and check your answers.

CPU (inside)

2 Reading

Read the text and study the diagram on page 8.

What is a computer?

Computers are electronic machines which can accept data in a certain form, process the data and give the results of the processing in a specified format as information.

5 Three basic steps are involved in the process. *First,* data is fed into the computer's memory. *Then,* when the program is run, the computer performs a set of instructions and processes the data. *Finally,* we can see the results (the 10 output) on the screen or in printed form (see the diagram on p. 8).

Information in the form of data and programs is known as **software**, and the electronic and mechanical parts that make up a computer 15 system are called **hardware**. A standard computer system consists of three main sections: the central processing unit (CPU), the main memory and the peripherals.

Perhaps the most influential component is the **central processing unit**. Its function is to 20 execute program instructions and coordinate the activities of all the other units. In a way, it is the 'brain' of the computer. The **main memory** holds the instructions and data which are currently being processed by the 25 CPU. The **peripherals** are the physical units attached to the computer. They include storage devices and input/output devices.

Storage devices (floppy, hard or optical disks) provide a permanent storage of both data and 30 programs. **Disk drives** are used to handle one or more floppy disks. **Input devices** enable

7

data to go into the computer's memory. The most common input devices are the **mouse** and the **keyboard**. **Output devices** enable us to extract the finished product from the system. For example, the computer shows the output on the **monitor** or prints the results onto paper by means of a **printer**.

On the rear panel of the computer there are several ports into which we can plug a wide range of peripherals – modems, fax machines, optical drives and scanners. 40

These are the main physical units of a computer system, generally known as the **configuration**. 45

35

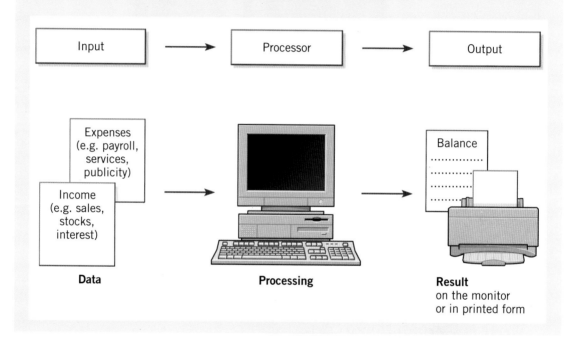

Use the information in the text and the diagram to help you match the terms in the box with the appropriate explanation or definition below.

a software   b peripheral devices   c monitor   d floppy disk   e hardware
f input   g port   h output   i central processing unit

1   The brain of the computer. ☐
2   Physical parts that make up a computer system. ☐
3   Programs which can be used on a particular computer system. ☐
4   The information which is presented to the computer. ☐
5   Results produced by a computer. ☐
6   Hardware equipment attached to the CPU. ☐
7   Visual display unit. ☐
8   Small device used to store information. Same as 'diskette'. ☐
9   Any socket or channel in a computer system into which an input/output
    device may be connected. ☐

3 Read and guess

Read these slogans or quotations, and say what computer element they refer to.

1 a 'Point and click here for power.'
  b 'Obeys every impulse as if it were an extension of your hand.'

     ....

2 a 'Displays your ideas with perfect brilliance.'
  b 'See the difference – sharp images and a fantastic range of colours.'

     ....

3 a 'I love this drive. It's quiet and fast.'
  b 'With this it's easy to back up your data before it's too late.'

     ....

4 a 'Power and speed on the inside.'
  b 'Let your computer's brain do the work.'

     ....

5 a '... a big impact on the production of text and graphics.'
  b 'Your choice: a laser powerhouse.'

     ....

4 Get ready for listening

Before listening, answer these questions.

1 Have you got a computer at home, school or work? What kind is it?
2 How often do you use it? What do you use it for?
3 What are the main components and features (the configuration) of your computer system?

5 Listening

A 🔊 **Listen to a short lecture given by John Griffiths, an expert on computer systems. As you listen, label the pictures below with the words in the box.**

> microcomputer (portable)   microcomputer (desktop PC)   mainframe   minicomputer

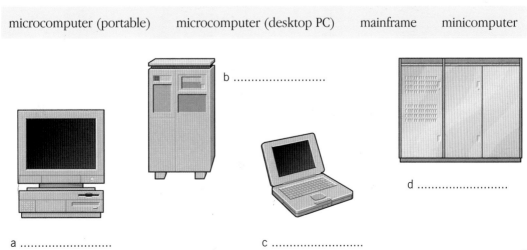

b ....

d ....

a ....

c ....

9

B ▄▄◉ **Listen again and choose the correct answer.**

1 According to the speaker:
   a a mainframe computer is less powerful than a minicomputer.
   b a mainframe is more powerful than a minicomputer.
   c a mainframe is not very powerful but can execute jobs very rapidly.

2 Mainframe computers are used by:
   a students and teachers in school.
   b executives and businessmen.
   c large organizations processing enormous amounts of data.

3 'Multitasking' means:
   a access to a minicomputer through terminals.
   b doing a number of tasks at the same time.
   c connection to a 'host' computer network so that many users have access to data and programs.

4 The most suitable computers for home use are:
   a mainframes.
   b minicomputers.
   c microcomputers (PCs).

5 The smallest computers are known as:
   a minicomputers.
   b desktop PCs.
   c laptops and notebook computers.

6 Follow-up: Minis and micros

Complete the text below with the words in the box.

systems	memory	task	terminals	desktop	CAD	applications

The first microcomputers, also known as (1) '...................................' PCs, were for single users only, and this clearly distinguished them from minicomputers. Another important difference was that 'minis' were much more powerful than 'micros': they could execute more than one (2) .... simultaneously and were used as file servers for (3) .... and workstations.

However, modern microcomputers have operating (4) .... and network facilities that can support many simultaneous users. Today, most personal computers have enough (5) .... to be used for word processing and business (6) .... Some PCs can even handle multitasking and (7) .... applications. As a result, the division between 'minis' and 'micros' is now disappearing.

Unit 3   *Inside the system*

1 Warm-up

A   **Read the advertisement and translate the technical specifications into your own language.**

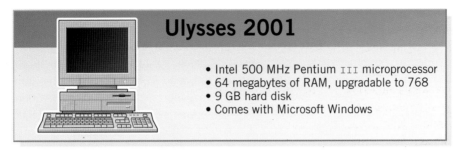

Ulysses 2001

- Intel 500 MHz Pentium III microprocessor
- 64 megabytes of RAM, upgradable to 768
- 9 GB hard disk
- Comes with Microsoft Windows

B   **Try to answer these questions. (If necessary look at the Glossary.)**

1   What is the main function of a microprocessor?
2   What unit of frequency is used to measure processor speed?
3   What does 'RAM' stand for?

2 Reading

A   **Read the text below and then sentences 1 to 8 on page 13. Decide if the sentences are true (T) or false (F), and rewrite the false ones to make them true.**

What's inside a microcomputer?

The nerve centre of a microcomputer is the central processing unit or CPU. This unit is built into a single microprocessor chip – an integrated circuit – which executes program instructions and supervises the computer's overall operation. The unit consists of three main parts:

i   the **control unit**, which examines the instructions in the user's program, interprets each instruction and causes the circuits and the rest of the components – disk drives, monitor, etc. – to be activated to execute the functions specified;

ii   the **arithmetic logic unit** (ALU), which performs mathematical calculations (+, –, etc.) and logical operations (and, or, etc.);

iii   the **registers**, which are high-speed units of memory used to store and control information. One of these registers is the program counter (PC) which keeps track of the next instruction to be performed in the main memory. Another is the instruction register (IR) which holds the instruction that is currently being executed (see Fig. 1.)

One area where microprocessors differ is in the amount of data – the number of bits – they can work with at a time. There are 8, 16, 32 and 64-bit processors. The computer's internal architecture is evolving so quickly that the new 64-bit processors are able to address 4 billion times more information than a 32-bit system (see Fig. 2).

The programs and data which pass through the central processor must be loaded into the **main memory** (also called the **internal memory**) in order to be processed. Thus, when the user runs an application, the microprocessor looks for it on secondary storage devices (disks) and transfers a copy of the application into the RAM area. RAM (random access memory) is temporary, i.e. its information is lost when the computer is turned off. However, the ROM section (read only memory) is permanent and contains instructions needed by the processor.

Most of today's computers have internal **expansion slots** that allow users to install adapters or expansion boards. Popular adapters include high-resolution graphics boards, memory expansion boards, and internal modems.

The power and performance of a computer is partly determined by the speed of its microprocessor. A **clock** provides pulses at fixed intervals to measure and synchronize circuits and units. The clock speed is measured in MHz (megahertz) and refers to the frequency at which pulses are emitted. For example, a CPU running at 500 MHz (500 million cycles per second) is likely to provide a very fast processing rate and will enable the computer to handle the most demanding applications.

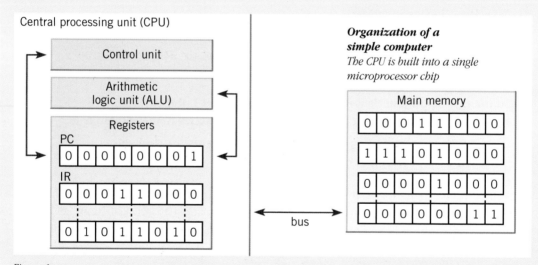

Figure 1

The new generation of processors

Figure 2 shows the 600 MHz Alpha microprocessor from Digital, with a 64-bit RISC implementation (Reduced Instruction Set Computing) architecture, providing lightning-fast performance.

Figure 2

Other popular platforms are:
- Intel's Pentium
- Apple, IBM and Motorola's PowerPC
- Sun's SuperSPARC
- Silicon Graphics/Mips R10000 and R5000.

1 The CPU directs and coordinates the activities taking place within the computer system. ☐
2 The arithmetic logic unit performs calculations on the data. ☐
3 32-bit processors can handle more information than 64-bit processors. ☐
4 A chip is an electronic device composed of silicon elements containing a set of integrated circuits. ☐
5 RAM, ROM and secondary storage are the components of the main memory. ☐
6 Information cannot be processed by the microprocessor if it is not loaded into the main memory. ☐
7 'Permanent' storage of information is provided by RAM (random access memory). ☐
8 The speed of the microprocessor is measured in megahertz. One MHz is equivalent to one million cycles per second. ☐

Contextual reference

B **What do the words in bold print refer to?**

1 ... **which** executes program instructions and supervises ... (line 4)
2 ... the instruction **that** is currently being executed. (line 23)
3 ... the amount of data – the number of bits – **they** can work with at a time. (line 26)
4 ... the microprocessor looks for **it** on ... (line 38)
5 ... **its** information is lost when the computer is turned off. (line 41)
6 ... expansion slots **that** allow users to install adapters or expansion boards. (line 47)

3 Language work: Relative clauses

Look at the HELP box and then complete the sentences below with suitable relative pronouns. Give alternative options if possible.

HELP box
Relative clauses

We can define people or things with a restrictive (defining) clause.

● *The teacher **who** is responsible for the computer centre has just arrived.*
We use the relative pronoun 'who' because it refers to a person. We could also use 'that'.

● *The microprocessor is a chip **which** processes the information provided by the software.*
We use the relative pronoun 'which' because it refers to a thing, not a person. We could also use 'that'.

● *The computer we saw at the exhibition runs at 600 MHz.*
Relative pronouns can be left out when they are not the subject of the relative clause.

1 That's the CPU .... I'd like to buy.
2 The microprocessor is a chip .... processes data and instructions.
3 The microprocessor coordinates the activities .... take place in the computer system.

4 Last night I met someone .... works for GM as a computer programmer.

5 A co-processor is a silicon chip .... carries out mathematical operations at a very high speed.

6 A megahertz is a unit of frequency .... is used to measure processor speed.

7 Here's the floppy disk .... you lent me!

4 Listening

A **Label this diagram with the correct terms.**

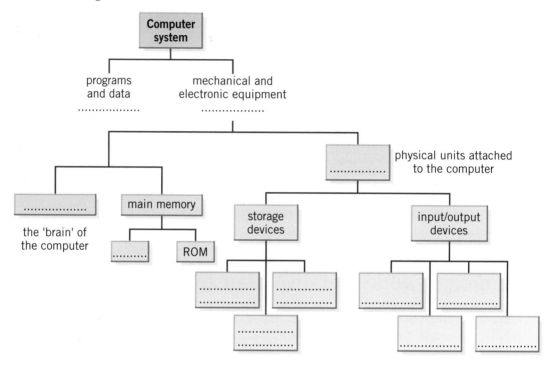

B **Compare your answers with a partner.**

C **Listen and check your answers.**

5 Reading

A **Read the text and complete it with the phrases in the box.**

All the information stored in the RAM is temporary
Microcomputers make use of two types of main memory
ROM chips have 'constant' information
the size of RAM is very important

Main memory: RAM and ROM

The main memory of a computer is also called the 'immediate access store', as distinct from any storage memory available on disks. (1) ....:.. .... : RAM and ROM, both contained in electronic chips connected to the main board of the computer.

RAM stands for 'random access memory' and is the working area of the computer, that is, the basic location where the microprocessor stores the required information. It is called 'random access' because the processor can find information in any cell or memory address with equal speed, instead of looking for the data in sequential order.

(2) .... , so it is lost when the machine is turned off. Therefore, if we want to use this information later on, we have to save it and store it on a disk. When running an application, the microprocessor finds its location in the storage device (the floppy or hard disk) and transfers a temporary copy of the application to the RAM area. Consequently, (3) .... if we want to increase the performance of a computer when several applications are open at the same time or when a document is very complex.

The RAM capacity can sometimes be expanded by adding extra chips. These are usually contained in single in-line memory modules or SIMMs, which are installed in the motherboard of the computer.

We can designate a certain amount of RAM space as a **cache** in order to store information that an application uses repeatedly. A RAM cache may speed up our work, but it means that we need enough internal memory or a special cache card.

ROM is an acronym for 'read only memory', which implies that the processor can read and use the information stored in the ROM chip, but cannot put information into it. (4) ...., including instructions and routines for the basic operations of the CPU. These instructions are used to start up the computer, to read the information from the keyboard, to send characters to the screen, etc. They cannot be changed and are not erased when the power is turned off. For this reason, the ROM section is also referred to as **firmware**.

A RAM chip

B **As we have seen, there are three types of memory used by computers: RAM, ROM and secondary storage. Look through this list of features and decide which type of memory they refer to.**

1 Any section of the main memory can be read with equal speed and ease.
2 It is available in magnetic, optical and video disks.
3 A certain amount of this memory can be designated as 'cache' memory to store information in applications that are used very frequently.
4 It stores basic operating instructions, needed by the CPU to function correctly.
5 Memory which can be expanded by adding SIMMs of 8 MB, 16 MB, 32 MB or other major increments.
6 Information is permanent and cannot be deleted.
7 You can save and store your documents and applications.

6 Vocabulary quiz

In groups of three, write answers to these questions. The winners are the group that answers the most questions correctly in four minutes.

1 What are the main parts of the CPU?
2 What is RAM?
3 What memory section is also known as 'firmware'?
4 What information is lost when the computer is switched off?
5 What is the typical unit used to measure RAM memory and storage memory?
6 What is the meaning of the acronym SIMM?
7 What is a megahertz?
8 What is the ALU? What does it do?
9 What is the abbreviation for 'binary digit'?
10 How can we store data and programs permanently?

7 Your ideal computer system

A **Make notes about the features of the computer that you would like to have.**

CPU: ....   Speed ....   Optical disk drives: ....
Minimum/maximum RAM: ....   Monitor: ....
Hard disk: ....   Software: ....

B **Now describe it to your partner.**

Useful expressions

It has got ...
It's very fast. It runs at ...
The standard RAM memory ... and it is expandable ...
The hard disk can hold ...
I need a SuperVGA monitor because ...
As for the Internet ...

Unit 4 *Bits and bytes*

1 Reading

A **With a partner, try to answer these questions.**

1 How many digits does a binary system use? What is a 'bit'?
2 What is the difference between binary notation and the decimal system? Give some examples.
3 What is a collection of eight bits called?
4 One kilobyte (1K) equals 1,024 bytes.
   Can you work out the value of these units?   (*kilo-*: one thousand)
   1 megabyte = ... bytes/1,024 kilobytes   (*mega-*: one million)
   1 gigabyte = ... bytes/1,024 megabytes   (*giga-*: one thousand million)
5 What does the acronym 'ASCII' stand for? What is the purpose of this code?

B **Now read the text to check your answers or to find the correct answer.**

Units of memory

Bits – basic units of memory

Information is processed and stored in computers as electrical signals. A computer contains thousands of electronic circuits connected by switches that can only be in one of two possible states: ON (the current is flowing through the wire) or OFF (the current is not flowing through the wire). To represent these two conditions we use **binary notation** in which 1 means ON and 0 means OFF. This is the only way a computer can 'understand' anything. Everything about computers is based upon this binary process. Each 1 or 0 is called a **binary digit** or **bit**.

Bytes and characters

1s and 0s are grouped into eight-digit codes that typically represent characters (letters, numbers and symbols). Eight bits together are called a **byte**. Thus, each character in a keyboard has its own arrangement of eight bits. For example, 01000001 for the letter A, 01000010 for B and 01000011 for C.

The ASCII code

The majority of computers use a standard system for the binary representation of characters. This is the American Standard Code for Information Interchange, known popularly as 'ASCII' (pronounced 'ask-key'). There are 256 different ways of combining 0 and 1 bits in a byte. So they can give us 256 different signals. However, the ASCII code only uses 128 bytes to represent characters. The rest of the bytes are used for other purposes.

The first 32 codes are reserved for characters such as the Return key, Tab, Escape, etc. Each letter of the alphabet, and many symbols (such as punctuation marks), as well as the ten numbers, have ASCII representations. What makes this system powerful is that these codes are standard.

Kilobytes, megabytes and gigabytes

In order to avoid astronomical figures and sums in the calculation of bytes, we use units such as kilobytes, megabytes and gigabytes. One kilobyte is 1,024 bytes (2^{10}) and it is represented as KB, or more informally as K. One megabyte is equivalent to 1,024 KB, and one gigabyte is 1,024 MB.

We use these units (KB, MB, GB) to describe the RAM memory, the storage capacity of disks and the size of any application or document.

C **Look at the illustrations and the captions below. Then fill in the blanks with the correct unit of memory.**

1 One .... represents one character.

2 One .... represents 1,024 characters (about a small page of text).

3 One .... represents 1,000,000 characters (about the text of this book).

4 One .... represents 1,000,000,000 characters (about 1,000 books in a library).

2 Word building

A **The table gives some prefixes commonly used in computer science. Knowing the meaning of these prefixes will help you understand new words.**

Prefix	Meaning	Examples
deci-	ten	*decimal, decimalize, decibel*
hexadeci-	sixteen	*hexadecimal*
kilo-	one thousand (1,000) (1,024 in binary: 2^{10})	*kilocycle, kilogram(me), kilowatt*
mega-	large; one million	*megahertz, megalith, megaton*
giga-	very large; one thousand million	*gigantic, gigabyte*
mini-	small	*minibus, minimum, minimize*
micro-	very small	*microfilm, microphone, microwave*
bi-	two	*bidirectional, bidimensional, binary*
tri-	three	*tripartite, tricycle, trilingual*
multi-	many	*multi-racial, multi-user, multitasking*
mono-	one	*monologue, monosyllable, monolingual*

B **Explain these expressions, taking into account the prefixes and root word.**

Example

the binary system

The binary system is a notation which uses two digits, 0 and 1.

1 a minicomputer
2 a microcomputer
3 the decimal system
4 the hexadecimal system
5 a multi-user configuration
6 a bidimensional chessboard
7 a tricycle
8 a monochrome computer
9 a CPU with 64 MB of RAM
10 a document of 3 kilobytes

3 Bits for pictures

A   **Read the questions and text and study the diagrams.**

Did you know that …

1   bits can also be used to code pictures?
2   the information displayed on the computer screen corresponds, dot by dot, with bits held in the main memory?
3   on colour systems, if you have 8 bits per primary colour, the palette of your computer can obtain 16.7 million colours?

Each tiny dot on the screen of a computer is called a picture element or **pixel**. Images and text are formed by combining a large number of pixels.

In a bit-mapped display, the dots displayed on the screen correspond, pixel by pixel, with bits in the main memory of the computer. The bits are held in an area of the memory called the 'refresh buffer' and are stored in groups that represent the horizontal and vertical position of the pixels on the screen and whether the pixels are on or off.

On monochrome systems, one bit in this 'map' represents one pixel on the screen and can be either 'on' or 'off' (black or white).

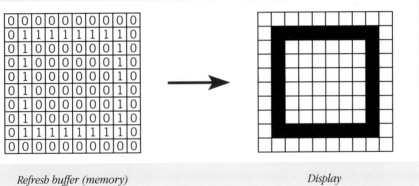

Refresh buffer (memory)   Display

On colour systems, each pixel is a certain combination of the three primary colours: red, green and blue. The total number of colours which can be shown on the screen is called the colour palette. The size of this palette depends on the graphics adaptor, a separate video card that converts the bits into visual signals. A graphics adaptor with 1 bit per primary colour can generate up to 8, or 2^3, colours, as you can see from the table on page 20. A graphics adaptor with 8 bits per primary colour can generate 16.7 million or $(2^3)^8$ colours.

Colour	Red	Green	Blue
black	0	0	0
blue	0	0	1
green	0	1	0
cyan	0	1	1
red	1	0	0
magenta	1	0	1
yellow	1	1	0
white	1	1	1

One bit per primary colour

B   **Using the information in the passage and the illustrations, match the terms in the box with the appropriate explanation or definition.**

> a pixel   b bit   c bit-mapped display
> d primary colours   e palette

1   The menu of colours available on a graphics system; its size depends on the hardware. ☐
2   Red, green and blue (RGB) in computers. ☐
3   The smallest element of a display surface. ☐
4   A display on the screen which corresponds, pixel by pixel, with bits stored in memory cells. ☐
5   The acronym for 'binary digit'; one of the digits (0 and 1) used in binary notation. ☐

C   **Translate the last paragraph (starting from 'On colour systems, …') into your language.**

   Do you understand the calculations made to obtain a palette of 16.7 million colours? (If you don't, ask a partner to explain them to you.)

Unit 5 *Buying a computer*

1 Before you listen

Name eight different items you can buy in a computer shop.

2 Listening

A    **You are going to hear two people making enquiries in a Macintosh computer shop. The shop assistant is telling them about the two models below. Listen and fill in the missing information.**

iMac
Processor speed   *266 MHz*
RAM standard   ....
Hard disk capacity   ....
Price   ....

Power Macintosh G3
Processor speed   ....
RAM standard   ....
Hard disk capacity   ....
Price   *£1,720*

B   **Now listen again and fill in the gaps below.**

Assistant:	Do you need any help?
Paul:	Um yes, we're looking for a personal computer. Have you got any fairly basic ones?
Assistant:	Yes, sure. If you'd like to come over here …
Paul:	What different (1) .... are there?

Assistant: At the moment we've got these two models: the iMac, which has a
(2) .... operating at 266 megahertz, and the Power Macintosh
G3 which has a processor (3) .... at 400 megahertz.

Sue: So the Power Macintosh G3 is the (4) .... one. And which one
has the most memory? I mean – which has the most RAM?

Assistant: Well, the iMac has 64 megabytes of (5) .... , which can be
(6) .... up to 256, and the Power Macintosh G3 has 128
megabytes which can be expanded up to (7) .... It all
depends on how much memory you think you're going to need.

3 Role play

**Work with a partner. One of you wants to buy a computer, the other is the
sales assistant. Ask and answer questions, using the information and
instructions below to help you.**

Products available	Processor/ Speed	Minimum/ Maximum RAM	Hard disk	Disk drives	Monitor	Price
Explora 700 Net PC	Mips R4700 300 MHz	32 MB expandable to 256	4 GB	Optional 3.5" drive	Super VGA compatible	£799
Toshiba portable	Pentium III 500 MHz	64 MB expandable to 256	10 GB	3.5" drive 32x CD	colour LCD DVD-Rom	£2,450
IBM Aptiva	AMD Athlon 700 MHz	128 MB expandable to 384	20 GB	3.5" drive DVD	XGA	£2,640
Polywell	AMD Athlon 700 MHz	128 MB expandable to 768	20 GB	3.5" drive CD/Zip	Super VGA	£2,330
Compaq	Pentium III 650 MHz	64 MB expandable to 768 MB	16 GB	Zip drive DVD	XGA	£2,580

Shop assistant   **Customer**

Greet the customer and offer help.

                    Ask to see some computers.

Show the customer some models.

                    Ask for details: processor, RAM, etc.

Describe the speed in megahertz and the main memory.

                    Ask about the hard disk.

Give explanations (MB storage capacity, etc.).

                    Ask about the monitor and other features.

Give the required information.

                    Ask the price.

Give the price and explain different ways of paying.

                    Decide to buy one/to think about it.

                    Thank the shop assistant and leave the shop.

4 Read and talk

A **Read the descriptions of the four people and the four computers below and on page 24. With a partner, choose the most suitable computer for each person. Give reasons for your choices.**

1 Daniel is a history student. He needs a computer to write essays, assignments and letters.
2 Sarah is the manager of an advertising company. She needs a powerful system which will work with optical disks and multimedia applications, integrating text and pictures with animation and voice annotations. Digitized images and sound occupy a lot of disk space.
3 Andy is a CAD engineer. His job involves computer-aided design, simulations and three-dimensional modelling. These applications require a lot of memory and a large drive.
4 Tanya is a sales representative. She needs a lightweight machine with which she can process orders and communicate with head office while she is on the road.

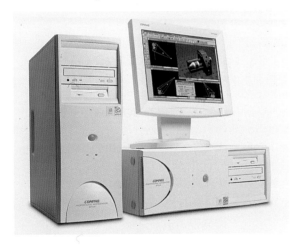

Digital Alpha workstation

- 600 MHz 64-bit Alpha microprocessor
- 128 MB RAM expandable up to 1.5 GB
- Hard disk capacity: 9 GB
- Supports several graphics formats
- Lets you attach any peripherals and link up to any network
- Allows you to handle your toughest technical, scientific and business-critical applications
- Supports Digital UNIX, Open VMS and Windows operating systems
- £4,049

HP Vectra

- Pentium processor running at 333 MHz
- 32 MB of RAM
- High density 3.5", 1.44 MB floppy disk drive
- 32x CD-ROM drive
- 3.2 GB hard disk
- Network card
- Standard keyboard and Microsoft mouse
- Windows
- £709

Compaq notebook

- 300 MHz Pentium processor with MMX technology
- 64 MB RAM
- 6 GB hard drive
- 3.5" floppy disk drive and CD-ROM drive
- Internal 56k modem
- 12.1" colour TFT display with high resolution
- Compaq trackball mouse
- Extended life NiMH battery
- Weighs only 6 lbs
- Windows comes pre-installed
- £2,399

Power Macintosh

- PowerPC processor at 400 MHz
- 128 MB of RAM expandable to 1 GB
- 1 MB of in-line cache on the processor card
- 16 MB of video RAM
- 12 GB hard disk
- 3.5" floppy drive, 24x CD-ROM and Zip unit
- Optional DVD-ROM drive
- Comes with AppleVision monitor, sound board, built-in microphone, and stereo speakers
- Mac OS with QuickTime (an extension that lets you play video and animation on the computer)
- £2,999

B   **Look back at the notes you made for Task 7 in Unit 3 (page 16) about your ideal computer system. What did you want?**

Read the descriptions of these computers again and choose the one that is closest to your ideal. Explain the reason for your choice.

5 Vocabulary tree

Designing vocabulary trees or networks can help you build up your own
mental 'maps' of vocabulary areas. Look at the list of terms in the box and
put each one in an appropriate place on the vocabulary tree below.
The first one has been done for you.

megahertz	gigabyte	expandable memory
kilobyte	firmware	binary system
ASCII code	megabyte	cache memory
SIMMs	binary digit	clock speed
bit-mapped display	basic instructions	pixel
permanent internal memory	computer 'brain'	processing rate
immediate access store		

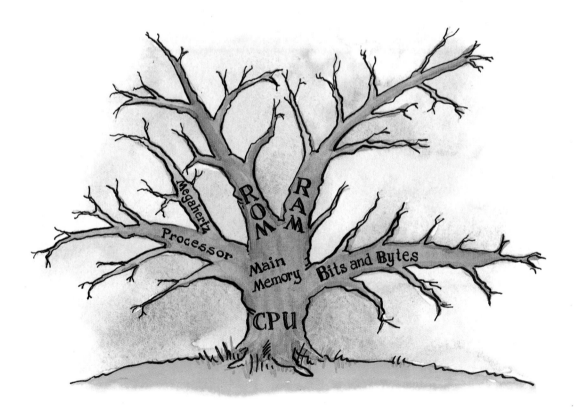

6 Writing

A friend has written to you asking you to recommend a computer that
suits their needs. Write a letter in reply, describing its technical features
and saying why you recommend it.

Input/output devices

Learning objectives

In this section you will learn how to:

- describe input and output devices
- identify important keys on a keyboard and explain their functions
- distinguish between facts and opinions in advertisements about peripherals (e.g. scanners)
- understand technical specifications given about monitors
- use different grammatical forms to give instructions, advice or warnings
- compare different types of printers, and choose one for yourself
- understand what sort of input/output devices are used by disabled people.

Unit 6 *Type and click!*

1 Interacting with your computer

Input devices are the pieces of hardware which allow us to enter information into the computer. The most common are the keyboard and the mouse. We can also interact with a computer by using one of these: a lightpen, a scanner, a trackball, a graphics tablet, a joystick or a voice recognition device.

Look at the illustrations and see if you can name them.

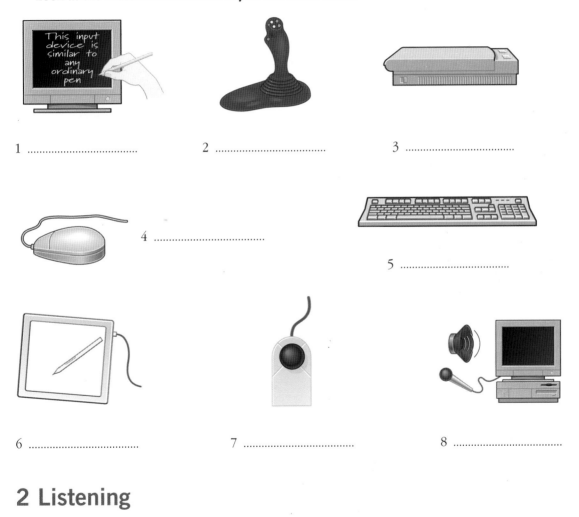

This input device is similar to any ordinary pen

1 ....

2 ....

3 ....

4 ....

5 ....

6 ....

7 ....

8 ....

2 Listening

A   🔊 **Listen to these descriptions of three input devices. What are they?**

    1 ....   2 ....   3 ....

B   **Check your answers with a partner.**

3 Language work

Look at the HELP box and then use the notes below to write a similar description of a joystick.

HELP box
Describing function

In Task 2, the mouse was described like this:
This is a device for controlling the cursor and selecting items on the screen.

for controlling describes what the mouse does *(for + -ing)*

There are several ways of describing function:

- *for + -ing (for controlling)*
- relative pronoun + verb *(which controls)*
- relative pronoun + *is used* + *to* + infinitive *(which/that is used to control)*
- used + *to* + infinitive *(used to control)*

Input device

Use: play games

The user takes hold of a lever to control/move the cursor around the screen.

---

4 Speaking

Work in pairs. Student A: turn to page 143 and Student B: turn to page 147.

5 About the keyboard

A **Look at the picture of a PC-compatible keyboard and identify these groups of keys.**

1 **Alphanumeric keys:** arranged in the same order as a typewriter.
2 **Function keys:** used by various programs to instruct the PC to perform specific tasks, such as Save, Copy, Cut, Paste, Help, etc.
3 **Numeric keypad:** set of numeric or editing keys. The Num Lock key is used to switch from numbers to editing functions.
4 **Editing keys:** cursor and other keys usually used within word processors to page up and down in a long document or to edit text (using Insert or Delete keys).
5 **Special keys:** used to issue commands or to produce alternative characters in key combinations, for example, the Alt key.

A PC-compatible keyboard

B   **Match these descriptions with the names of keys on the right. Then find them on the keyboard.**

1   A long key at the bottom of the keyboard. Each time it is pressed, it produces a blank space. (= ....)

2   It moves the cursor to the beginning of a new line. It is also used to confirm commands. (= ....)

3   It stops a program without losing the information from the main memory. Sometimes its use depends on the applications. (= ....)

4   It works in combination with other keys to produce special characters or specific actions. (= ....)

5   It removes the character on the left of the cursor or any selected text. (= ....)

6   It produces UPPER-CASE characters (or the upper-case character of the key). (= ....)

7   It produces upper-case letters, but it does not affect numbers and symbols. (= ....)

8   It moves the cursor horizontally to the right for a fixed number of spaces (in tabulations and data fields). (= ....)

9   They are used to move the cursor, as an alternative to the mouse. (= ....)

arrow keys

return

caps lock

shift

tab

escape

space bar

backspace

alt

C **Computer systems may have different keyboard options. Here is an example. If we enter the Key Caps menu on a Macintosh in Courier and then press the Option key, we obtain the following symbols on the screen:**

Identify these symbols on the keyboard.

1 slash
2 not equal to
3 plus and minus
4 trademark

5 yen sign
6 copyright
7 number
8 registered trademark

6 Reading

A **Try to answer these questions.**

1 How is the mouse connected to the computer?
2 What does the mouse pointer look like on the screen?
3 What are the functions of the mouse buttons?
4 What are the advantages of a computer mouse over a keyboard?

Read the text to check your answers or to find the right answers.

Point and click!

Typically, a mouse is a palm-sized device, slightly smaller than a pack of cards. On top of the mouse there are one or more buttons for communicating with the computer. A 'tail' or wire extends from the mouse to a connection on the back of the computer.

The mouse is designed to slide around on your desktop. As it moves, it moves an image on the screen called a **pointer** or **mouse cursor**. The pointer usually looks like an arrow or I-bar, and it mimics the movements of the mouse on your desktop.

What makes the mouse especially useful is that it is a very quick way to move around on a screen. Move the desktop mouse half an inch and the screen cursor will leap four inches. Making the same movements with the arrow keys takes much longer. The mouse also issues instructions to the computer very quickly. Point to an available option with the cursor, **click** on the mouse, and the option has been chosen.

Mice are so widely used in graphics applications because they can do things that are difficult, if not impossible, to do with keyboard keys. For example, the way you move an image with a mouse is to put the pointer on the object you want to move, press the mouse button and **drag** the image from one place on the screen to another. When you have the image where you want it, you release the mouse button and the image stays there. Similarly, the mouse is used to **grab** one corner of the image (say a square) and stretch it into another shape (say a rectangle). Both of these actions are so much more difficult to perform with a keyboard that most graphics programs require a mouse.

The buttons on the mouse are used to select items at which the mouse points. You position the pointer on an object on the screen, for example, on a menu or a tool in a paint program, and then you press the mouse button to 'select' it. Mice are also used to load documents into a program: you put the pointer on the file name and **double-click** on the name – that is, you press a mouse button twice in rapid succession.

(Adapted from *Your First Computer*, A. Simpson, Sybex, 1992)

B   **Here are some basic mouse actions. Match the terms in the box with the explanations below.**

a click   b double-click   c drag

1   Position the pointer on something, then rapidly press and release the mouse button twice. (You do this to load a program, open a document or select text or graphics.) ☐

2   Position the pointer on something, hold down the mouse button and move the mouse to the desired position, then release the button. (You do this to move an image to a new location on the screen.) ☐

3   Position the pointer on something, then press and release the mouse button. (You do this to place the insertion point, to choose an option, or to close a window.) ☐

Unit 7 *Capture your favourite image*

1 Scanners: The eyes of your computer

Use the information in the text and the illustration to answer these questions.

1 What is a scanner? Give a definition in your own words.
2 How does a colour scanner work?

What does a scanner do?

A scanner converts text or pictures into electronic codes that can be manipulated by the computer.

In a flatbed scanner, the paper with the image is placed face down on a glass screen similar to a photocopier. Beneath the glass are the lighting and measurement devices. Once the scanner is activated, it reads the image as a series of dots and then generates a digitized image that is sent to the computer and stored as a file. The manufacturer usually includes software which offers different ways of treating the scanned image.

A colour scanner operates by using three rotating lamps, each of which has a different coloured filter: red, green and blue. The resulting three separate images are combined into one by appropriate software.

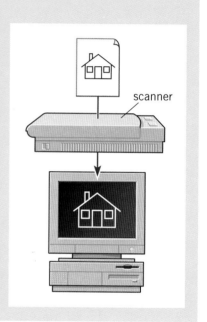

scanner

A scanner 'sees' images and translates them into a form that can be understood by the computer

What do you think are the benefits of using scanners in business?

2 Listening

Listen to the conversation between Vicky Cameron, an Information Technology (IT) lecturer, and one of her students, and complete these notes.

1 The technology used in scanners is similar to that used in ....
2 A laser beam reads the image in ....
3 The image is then ....
4 Text is scanned with ....
5 Flatbed scanners can scan ....
6 Slide scanners are used to scan ....
7 Hand-held scanners are used for capturing ....

3 Facts and opinions

A **Read the advertisements below and underline what you think are facts and circle the opinions. Then write them in the table on page 34.**

Facts are 'real' objective information. *Opinions* usually include emotive words, positive/negative phrases and subjective (persuasive) statements.

HELP box

- **dpi:** dots per inch
- **9" × 15":** scanning area measured in inches
- **JPEG:** Joint Photographic Experts' Group – a standard format in image compression. With JPEG, your images can be compressed to 1/50th of normal size, resulting in a substantial saving of disk space and time

1

ColourScan XR
from Sunrise

The ColourScan XR from Sunrise is a flatbed scanner with 600 dpi of resolution and 9" x 15" of scanning area.

Think of the possibilities.

You can enter data and graphic images directly into your applications – word processors or databases. You can get crisp, clean scans for colour compositions, video and animation work.

It comes complete with its own image-capture software which allows for colour and grey retouching. And it's easy to use. What more could you want for only £616? It couldn't be cheaper.

In the field of flatbeds, the ColourScan XR is a clear winner.

ColourScan XR

2

ScanPress 800

The ScanPress 800 is a self-calibrating, flatbed scanner with 800 dpi of resolution. You can scan from black and white to 24-bit colour. The package includes a hardware accelerator for JPEG compression and decompression. JPEG technology saves disk space by compressing images up to 50 to 1.

In creating ScanPress 800, the manufacturers have chosen the highest technology to give you the best scans with the least effort. It produces images with high colour definition and sharpness. And it comes with OCR software and Adobe Photoshop, so you can manipulate all the images you capture.

This is a fantastic machine you will love working with. And at only £1,037 it is an excellent investment.

	ColourScan XR	*ScanPress 800*
Facts	Flatbed scanner 600 dpi of resolution	Self-calibrating, flatbed scanner
Opinions	You can get crisp, clean scans	The highest technology

B **In small groups, compare your answers and decide:**

1 which text has got more persuasive language?
2 which text is more factual or objective?

4 Language work: Comparatives and superlatives

Apart from catchy slogans and other persuasive techniques, advertisements often use the comparatives and superlatives of adjectives and adverbs. Read the following examples from advertisements. What can you say from these examples about how comparatives and superlatives are formed?

1 … only ten times faster.
2 It couldn't be cheaper.
3 The manufacturers have chosen the highest technology …
4 The cleverest personal scanner …
5 The most revolutionary computer peripheral …
6 The best scans with the least effort …
7 Flatbed scanners are more accurate than …
8 Now you can edit your documents more easily than ever, and they'll look better than ever too with …

5 Word building

The class of a word can often be changed by adding a suffix. For example, if *-er* is added to the verb *scan* (and the 'n' is doubled) we get the noun *scanner*.

Common adjectival suffixes are: *-ing, -y, -able, -ible, -ive, -al, -ed, -ful*
Common noun suffixes are: *-er, -or, -ion, -tion, -ation, -ment, -ness, -ity, -ant, -logy*

Put the words in the box into the correct column below.

> computer   self-calibrating   easy   resolution   sharpness   information
> printed   personal   capable   compression   technology   calculator
> useful   assistant   expensive   possibility   reducible   investment

Adjectives

....

....

....

....

....

....

....

....

....

Nouns

....

....

....

....

....

....

....

....

....

6 Advertisement: A scanner

Some of the adjectives have been left out of this persuasive advertisement.
Read it and complete it with words from the box.

> stunning   affordable   wide   excellent   complete   easy-to-use

The GT-7000 provides amazing quality with powerful, (1) .... software and hardware at a very (2) .... price. Using a combination of EPSON Advanced Scanning Technologies, the GT-7000 provides (3) .... quality whether scanning text documents, photos or film.

The EPSON START Button takes the complexity out of scanning. Simply press this button once and your photo or document is scanned and inserted into the software package of your choice ready for editing, printing or publishing.

Included with the GT-7000 is a (4) .... range of bonus software to help with home and business scanning, printing and publishing, allowing you to create

(5) .... posters, letters, flyers and Web pages.

The GT-7000 is also available as the GT-7000 Photo scanner (6) .... with advanced film adapter unit.

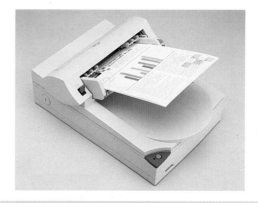

Unit 8 *Viewing the output*

1 Read and think

We interact with computers by entering instructions and data into them. After this information has been processed internally, we can see the results on the **visual display unit** or **VDU**. To obtain a permanent copy of these results, we can use plotters, printers or video recorders. In this interactive process with the computer, the screen plays an important part.

Describe the screen of your computer to another student. Use these questions to help you.

- Is it a monochrome or a colour monitor?
- What size is it?
- Does it produce a high quality image?

2 Reading

A **Read the text and try to guess the meaning of any new words in the box below. Refer to the Glossary if necessary.**

> dot   pixel   display   resolution   cathode ray tube   electron beam
> scan (verb)   hertz   refresh rate   flicker   bit-mapped   visualize

The monitor

The characters and pictures that we see on the screen are made up of dots, also called picture elements (pixels). The total number of pixels in which the display is divided both horizontally and vertically is known as the **resolution**. If the number of pixels is very large, we obtain a high resolution display and therefore a sharp image. If the number of pixels is small, a low resolution is produced.

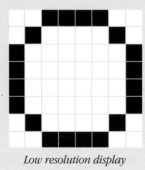

Low resolution display

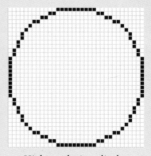

High resolution display

Typical resolutions are 640 × 480 or 1,024 × 768 pixels. The diagrams on page 36 show how pixel density affects the image: a larger number of pixels gives a much clearer image.

The **cathode ray tube** of the monitor is very similar to that of a TV set. Inside the tube there is an electron beam which scans the screen and turns on or off the pixels that make up the image. The beam begins in the top left corner, and scans the screen from left to right in a continuous sequence, similar to the movement of our eyes when we read, but much faster. This sequence is repeated 50, 60 or 75 times per second, depending on the system. If the rate of this repetition is low, we can perceive a flickering, unsteady screen, which can cause eye fatigue. However, a fast-moving 75 Hz 'refresh rate' eliminates this annoying flicker.

What we see on the screen is created and stored in an area of RAM, so that there is a memory cell allocated to each pixel. This type of display is called **bit-mapped**. On monochrome monitors, bits 0 are visualized as white dots, and bits 1 as black dots.

On colour displays, there are three electron guns at the back of the monitor's tube. Each electron gun shoots out a beam of electrons; there is one beam for each of the three primary colours: red, green and blue. These electrons strike the inside of the screen which is coated with substances called phosphors that glow when struck by electrons. Three different phosphor materials are used – one each for red, green and blue. To create different colours, the intensity of each of the three electron beams is varied.

The monitor is controlled by a separate circuit board, known as the display adaptor, which plugs into the motherboard of the computer. Different boards drive different types of displays. For example, the **VGA** (video graphics array) card has become a standard for colour monitors.

Portable computers use a flat **liquid-crystal display** (LCD) instead of a picture tube. An LCD uses a grid of crystals and polarizing filters to show the image. The crystals block the light in different amounts to generate the dots in the image.

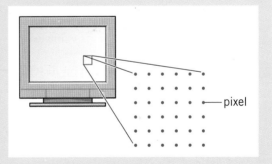

Each dot on the screen is a pixel

B   **Read the text again and answer these questions.**

1   According to the writer, what is the importance of 'pixel resolution'?
2   Which unit of frequency is used to measure the refresh rate of a monitor?
3   In the writer's opinion, why can a low refresh rate produce eye fatigue?
4   What substance is hit by electrons in a monitor?
5   What is the standard display system for many PCs?
6   What does 'LCD' stand for? What type of computers use LCD displays?

3 Writing

A **Tables often include abbreviations and technical words that are not easy to understand. Look at this table and the explanation of Monitor A's specifications.**

	CRT size	*CRT face*	*Pixel res.*	*Visual display*	*Refresh rate*	*Tilt-and-swivel*	*Other features*
Monitor A Superview	16"	flat	870 × 640	256 shades of grey	60 Hz	✓	anti-glare filter
Monitor B Paintview	19"	flat	1,024 × 768	32,000 colours	75 Hz	✓	video card

The specifications of Superview (Monitor A) may be explained like this:

1 This monochrome monitor has a 16-inch screen.
2 This display system has a resolution of 870 × 640 pixels that gives you enough quality for graphics.
3 It offers 256 shades of grey.
4 It has a 60 hertz refresh rate. (This is quite low, so it will probably produce a flickering, unsteady image.)
5 A tilt-and-swivel stand is used to move the monitor up, down and around so that the angle can be adjusted for each user.
6 The anti-glare filter helps eliminate eye fatigue and electromagnetic radiation.

B **Use this example to help you describe Monitor B.**

4 Listening

▣◉ **Tony Clark, a lecturer in computer ergonomics, is talking to some students about health and safety in a computer classroom. Listen and complete the sentences below. Then decide where they should go in the pictures on page 39. Write the number of each in the correct place.**

1 You should get a good chair, one that ....
2 Position the keyboard ....
3 Position the monitor .... eye level, or just ....
4 A tilt-and-swivel display lets you ....
5 You should stay an arm's length away from ....
6 If you work in a room with a lot of computers, sit ....

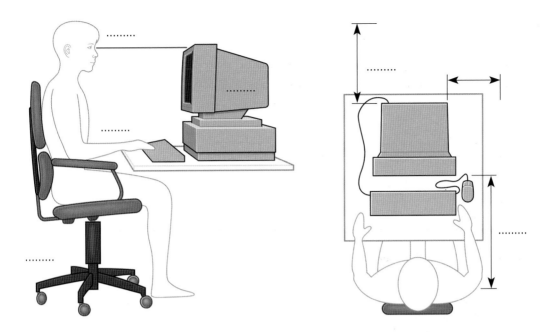

5 Language work: Instructions and advice

Look at the HELP box and then rewrite the sentences below about what you should do to protect your eyes. Use modal auxiliary verbs in your sentences.

HELP box
Instructions and advice

Imperatives
Position *your keyboard at the same height as your elbows.*
Don't use *a monitor that is fuzzy or distorts the image.*

Should/ought to
*You **should** position your keyboard at the same height as your elbows. = You **ought to** ...*
*You **shouldn't** use a monitor that is fuzzy or distorts the image. = You **ought not (oughtn't)** to use ...*

---

1 Do not stare at the screen for long periods of time.
2 Avoid placing the monitor so that it reflects a source of bright light, such as a window.
3 Keep the screen clean to prevent distorting shadows.
4 If you work in an office with a large number of computers, don't sit too close to the sides or backs of the monitors.
5 Buy a protective filter that cuts down the ELF (extremely low frequency) emissions.

Unit 9 *Choosing a printer*

1 Reading

A **How many kinds of printers can you think of? Make a list.**

B **Read the text below and label these types of printers.**

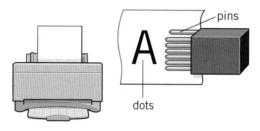

*The resolution depends on
the number of pins (9 or 24)*
1 ....

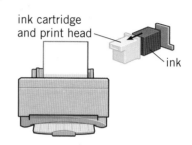

*The quality (resolution) of the images
ranges from 180 to 720 dots per inch (dpi)*
2 ....

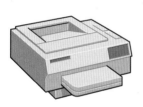

*Provides high quality
output – a resolution
of 600/1,200 (dpi)*
3 ....

*Provides the highest
resolution – more than
2,000 dpi*
4 ....

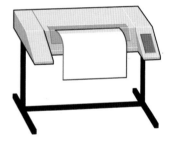

*Provides high quality for
linework (like lines and
curves)*
5 ....

Types of printers

Printing is the final stage in creating a document. That is the purpose of the printers joined to your computing equipment. *Since* the results you can obtain with different types of printers will vary substantially, here is a guide to help you decide which one is most suitable for your needs.

To begin with, it must be taken into account that printers vary in cost, speed, print quality and other factors such as noise or compatibility. In fact, printing technology is evolving so quickly that there is always a printer for every application or personal requirement.

Dot-matrix printers use pins to print the dots required to shape a character. They print text and graphics and nowadays some of them can print up to 450 characters per second (cps); *however,* they produce relatively low resolution output – 72 or 144 dots per inch. This level of quality, *while* suitable for preliminary drafts, is not recommended for reports or books that have a wide audience. They are slower than laser printers *but* much cheaper.

One common type of non-impact printer is an **ink-jet** printer. It operates by projecting small ink droplets onto paper to form the required image. This type of printer is quite fast, silent *and* not so expensive as a laser printer. *Nevertheless,* you can expect high quality results *because* there are some ink-jet printers on the market with a resolution of 720 dpi. **Bubble-jet** printers work the same way.

Laser printers produce output at great speed and with a very high resolution of 600/1,200 dpi. They scan the image with a laser beam and transfer it to paper with a special ink powder. They are constantly being improved. In terms of speed and image quality they are preferred by experts for different reasons: they have a wider range of scalable fonts, they can emulate different language systems, they can produce graphics, and they have many other advantages. It goes without saying that they are still expensive.

We must not forget to mention **thermal** printers. They use heat, a special kind of paper and electrosensitive methods. They are silent and considered to be inexpensive. However, some colour models that emulate HP (Hewlett Packard) plotters cost too much to be included in the same category.

Photosetters can be regarded as an attractive alternative. They do not print on regular paper, *but* on photographic paper or microfilm. They can produce output with a resolution of over 2,000 dots per inch. *In addition*, they are extremely fast. *Although* they produce the highest quality output, they have one important drawback: they are the most expensive.

Finally, **plotters** are a special kind of printer. Plotters use ink and fine pens held in a carriage to draw very detailed designs on paper. They are used for construction plans, engineering drawings and other technical illustrations.

C   **Read the text again and complete this table with the most relevant information. Then compare your notes with a partner.**

Type of printer	Technical specifications and other features
Dot-matrix	....
Ink-jet	....
Laser	....
Thermal	....
Photosetter	....
Plotter	....

2 Discourse cohesion

Reference signals

A   **Read the text and say what the** boxed **words refer to.**

Printing is the final stage in creating a document. [That] is the purpose of the printers joined to your computing equipment. Since the results you can obtain with different types of printers will vary substantially, here is a guide to help you decide which [one] is most suitable for your needs.

5 To begin with, it must be taken into account that printers vary in cost, speed, print quality and other factors [such] as noise or compatibility. In fact, printing technology is evolving so quickly that there is always a printer for every application or personal requirement.

Dot-matrix printers use pins to print the dots required to shape a character. [They] 10 print text and graphics and nowadays some of [them] can print up to 450 characters per second (cps).

Linking devices

B **In pairs, look at the text in Task 1 again and put the words in *italics* into one of the columns in the table below.**

Indicating addition	Contrasting	Sequencing	Reason/cause

C **Write a short text about the pros and cons of a printer or printers you use. Use some linking devices from the list above. Write about these aspects: type, cost, speed, noise, output quality, resident fonts.**

3 Listening

A Listen to the radio interview and tick (✓) the statements about ink-jet printers that are true.

1 Ink-jet printers are quieter than dot-matrix printers. ☐
2 Ink-jet printers are cheaper than dot-matrix printers. ☐
3 Ink-jet printers are not real competition for laser printers. ☐
4 Ink-jet printers can easily print on envelopes, labels and transparencies. ☐
5 Ink-jet colour printers use four inks: magenta, yellow, cyan and black. ☐
6 Ink-jets are ideal for workgroups and large businesses. ☐

B Listen again and, with the help of a partner, correct the statements that are not true.

An ink-jet printer

4 Scan reading: Quiz

Read the advertisements for printers below, and then, with your partner, answer the questions. See who in your group/class can finish first.

1 How many laser printers are advertised here?
2 Is there a printer that operates by spraying ink droplets onto paper?
3 Which laser printer offers the highest resolution, or output quality?
4 Which printer is the most expensive?
5 Which one would you recommend to a friend who does not have much money?
6 Which one has more internal fonts?
7 A printer language is software that tells printers how to print a document. Can you find two types of laser printer languages?
8 What connectivity features are offered by the Turbo Laser Writer QR?
9 A very common feature in advertisements is the use of abbreviations. Find the abbreviations for these expressions: *dots per inch, characters per second, pages per minute, small computer system interface* and *liquid-crystal display*.

Turbo Laser Writer QR

Workgroup laser printer. 15 pages per minute. 600 dpi for graphics. 36 MB of RAM. Includes Adobe PostScript and Hewlett Packard PCL printer languages. 75 resident fonts. Connectivity: one bi-directional parallel port, one LocalTalk port, and one Ethernet port for networks. 12 month warranty.

£1,150

Stylus Dot-matrix Printer

Dot-matrix printer with 24 pins. Prints text and graphics. 450 cps. Compatible special interface. Free unlimited hotline support for our customers. One year on-site maintenance.

£179

COLOUR POSTSCRIPT PRINTER

Colour printer. 40 Adobe PostScript fonts. 36 MB RAM with a SCSI Interface for an optional 20 MB hard disk. Parallel, serial and AppleTalk interfaces. HP plotter emulation. Thermal printing system. 30-day money-back guarantee and 1 year's on-site parts and labour.

£2,249

Crystal Laser Printer II

14 pages per minute. **6 MB RAM.**
Two 200 sheet selectable input trays.
LCD display.
80 internal scalable fonts.
A resolution of 1,200 dpi.
Comes with PostScript language and PCL (printer control language). **£999**
Telephone hotline support.

COLOUR INK-JET

Stunning Plug & Play colour printer. Brilliant photo quality (up to 720 dpi) and fast-drying ink. Produces 8 pages per minute in plain text and 4 ppm in colour. 150 page paper tray. Fast, friendly service.

£210

Micro Laser XT

Personal laser printer. 5 pages per minute. 4 MB RAM expandable to 64 MB. Parallel interface. 200 sheet input tray. 35 resident fonts. One-year on-site maintenance. Prints on a wide range of materials and sizes.

£649

5 Language work: Revision of comparison

A   **Study the sentences below and do the following:**

• draw a circle around comparatives and a rectangle around superlatives
• identify two special cases.

1   Dot-matrix printers are cheaper than laser printers.
2   A photosetter is the fastest output device.
3   A thermal wax printer is more expensive than a monochrome laser printer.
4   The Micro Laser XT is the most reliable of all.
5   Personal laser printers cost less than ordinary laser printers. They
     also weigh less and require less space.
6   My printer has more resident fonts than yours.
7   This printer offers laser quality at a lower price.
8   Monochrome printers operate faster than colour ones.
9   Dot-matrix printers are too slow.
10 Dot-matrix printers are not quick enough.

B   **Look at the advertisements on page 43 again and compare the printers.**
Talk about their: speed, memory, fonts, emulations, resolution, service,
price, noise. Use adjectives from the box below.

fast	slow	high/low quality	noisy	quiet	cheap
expensive	easy	difficult	simple	powerful	reliable
adaptable	expandable	compatible with			

6 Describing your ideal printer

Describe to your partner the characteristics of the printer you would like to use.
Give reasons.

Unit 10   *I/O devices for the disabled*

1 Adaptive technology

Working in pairs or small groups, look at the pictures and discuss these questions. Use the phrases in the box to help you.

1 What sort of difficulties do you think are experienced by computer users with limitations of vision or mobility?
2 What types of devices could be helpful to blind users?
3 How can a person with mobility limitations communicate with a computer? Think of possible tools or solutions.

Key words

blind person	adapted keyboard
magnification software	on-screen keyboard
Braille printer	voice recognition system
adaptive switch	screen-pointing device
optical head pointer	speech synthesis system
motor-impaired person	

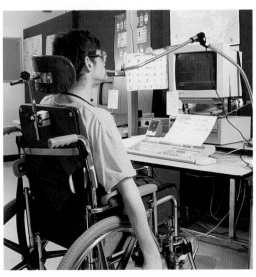

2 Reading

A   **Read the text below and find:**

1   two examples of speech synthesis systems
2   the kind of software which is recommended for someone with partial vision
3   the speed of the Juliet Braille printer
4   the ways adaptive switches can be activated
5   the function of voice recognition devices
6   the devices used by the disabled person at the Center for the Handicapped in Seattle
7   how the blind student (in the photo) interacts with the machine
8   how Bob Love enters information into the computer.

Computers for the disabled

Sal has all the necessary qualities for becoming a good telemarketer.* He's bright, outgoing and persistent. He is also blind. Phyllis wants to hire him, but she has some concerns. How will
5 he be able to use the company's database if he can't see the monitor? How will he read office correspondence? And more important, what will it cost the company to adapt the workplace to accommodate him?

10 Phyllis *must* accommodate him, since her company is in the US, and therefore subject to the Americans with Disabilities Act or ADA.† But she needn't worry. The latest adaptive technology for personal computers provides a cost-effective
15 way to allow Sal and workers with other disabilities to do their job with independence.

The first task in adding adaptive technology to a computer is to determine the specific needs of the disabled worker in question. To work effectively, most **blind users** need to have their 20
computers adapted with technologies such as speech synthesis, magnification, Braille and OCR. One example of a speech-synthesis system is VertPro from TeleSensory. This product can read MS-DOS-based word processors, databases, 25
spreadsheets, and other text-based software. Window Bridge from Syntha-Voice can verbalize both MS-DOS and Windows-based applications.

For someone with limited but usable vision, a software magnification package may be 30
appropriate. Magnification software can enlarge text appearing on the screen by up to 16 times.

A disabled person using a voice command-activated computer at the Center for the Handicapped in Seattle. He operates the system with a headset microphone, muscle switches and a joystick control

A blind student using an adapted keyboard, in the presence of his tutor. The headphones and a screen reading program allow him to hear the text from the screen

For Braille output, the Juliet printer from Enabling Technologies interfaces to any standard serial or parallel port. This printer can emboss Braille on both sides of a page at a speed of 40 characters per second. The Reading Edge OCR from Xerox Imaging Systems and the Arkenstone Open Book Unbound from Arkenstone can read printed material to blind people and send the text to a PC.

To adapt equipment for **motor-impaired workers** unable to type on a standard keyboard, you can employ adapted keyboards, head pointers and Morse code systems.

The user can also have an external adaptive switch to select menu choices or virtual keys from an on-screen keyboard. Adaptive switches come in a variety of forms that can be activated by eye movements, breath control or any other reliable muscle movement.

Another way of controlling computers is via a Morse code system. Such a system consists of adaptive switches and software for people who can't type on a full keyboard but have the ability to physically push at least one key.

Voice-recognition systems permit people to issue verbal commands to a computer to perform data entry.

Bob Love was born with no arms. He uses an overlay keyboard with his feet and the computer and monitor on the floor. The key overlays give a much larger surface for each key

(Adapted from 'Computers for the disabled', Joseph J. Lazzaro, *BYTE Magazine*, June 1993)

* Someone who markets products by phone.

† This makes it illegal for employers to discriminate against people with disabilities.

B   **Match the terms in the box with the explanations below.**

| a disability | b Braille | c port |
| d interface | e speech synthesizer | f Morse code |

1   a system of writing and reading (using raised dots) for blind people, to enable them to read by touch □

2   a socket to connect I/O devices □

3   incapacity □

4   a system of dots and dashes, or short and long sounds, representing letters of the alphabet and numbers □

5   a hardware device used in conjunction with a screen reader program to convert screen contents into spoken words □

6   channels and control circuits which allow different parts of a computer to communicate with one another. It also refers to the part of the system that allows a user to interact with programs □

3 Language work: Noun phrases

A **Look at the HELP box and then the noun phrases 1 to 7. Decide what type of modifier(s) is/are placed before the 'head' in each case.**

Types of modifiers

a adjective
b participle
c 's genitive
d noun

1 disabled worker
2 rehabilitation engineer
3 employee's abilities
4 external adaptive switch
5 Windows-based applications
6 pointing device
7 speech synthesizer

B **Explain the following noun phrases.**

Examples

memory chips   *chips of memory*
disk controller   *a device which controls*
                  the disk drive

1 screen reader
2 printing devices
3 company's database
4 adapted keyboards
5 magnification program
6 eye movements

HELP box
Noun phrases

In describing a noun phrase, we can distinguish two components:

● the head

● the modifier – notably adjectives and nouns. Thus:
  – *compatible*   *computer*
    modifier   head
  – *machine*   *code*
    modifier   head

We have the following range of modifiers:

● adjectives
  I like this portable computer.
  – a computer which is portable

● participles
  I like this drawing and painting program.
  – a program that draws and paints
  I like this pocket-sized computer.
  – a computer that fits into your pocket

● 's genitive
  I like the director's computer.
  – the computer which belongs to the director

● nouns
  I like this colour scanner.
  – a scanner which works in colour

4 Listening

A ▭◉ **Mike Hartley is a director of the Adaptive Technology Project for the Blind in Washington, DC. Listen to this interview with him in which he discusses the needs of blind computer users and make notes.**

- Work he's involved in: ....
- Minimum configuration required to meet the needs of these workers:
    Processor: ....
    RAM: ....
- Expansion slots: ....
- Specific technologies (input/output devices): ....
- Companies that are developing adaptive equipment: ....

B **Compare your notes in pairs.**

C ▭◉ **Listen again and complete your notes.**

5 Writing

Write a letter to Mike Hartley asking for information about computers for the disabled. Make sure you include the following points.

- Begin by saying why you're writing:
    I am writing to …
- Ask for information about specific I/O equipment for deaf, blind and motor-disabled workers:
    I would like to know …
    Ask for a free handbook about how to add adaptive technology to personal computers:
    I would be very grateful if …
- End the letter appropriately:
    I look forward to hearing from you soon.
    Yours sincerely …

Storage devices

Learning objectives

In this section you will learn how to:

- ask and answer questions about floppy and hard disks
- describe different types of storage devices
- locate specific information in texts about optical disks
- use technical vocabulary connected with disks and drives
- give advice and make recommendations about disks and drives.

Unit 11 *Floppies*

1 Warm-up

Look at the photograph and answer the questions.

1 What is the person doing?
2 What do people use floppies (also called 'diskettes') for?

*A floppy drive spins at
360 revolutions per minute*

2 Protect your floppies

A Match the instructions to the pictures.

1 Protect your floppies against high temperatures. ☐
2 Remember to block the disk if you want to be sure that information
   is not changed or erased by accident. ☐
3 Do not put heavy objects on top of the disk. ☐
4 Magnetic fields can damage the information stored on disks.
   Don't leave them near the telephone. ☐
5 Keep disks away from water and humidity. ☐
6 Do not touch the magnetized surface under the metallic cover. ☐

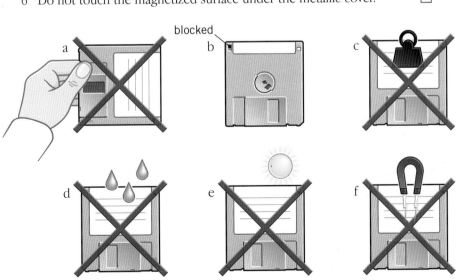

B In pairs, tell each other what you must or mustn't do to protect your disks.

Example

You mustn't leave them on top of your computer.

1 in a protective case
2 into the disk drive very carefully
3 near strong magnetic fields
4 at a temperature of between 10°C and 52°C
5 bend or fold the disk

3 Listening

Sue is in a shop. Listen to the conversation and answer these questions.

1 What type of disks did Sue want to buy – hard or floppy?
2 Did she mention a particular make of disk?
3 What is the storage capacity of high density disks?
4 How much was a pack of ten formatted disks?
5 Which disks did she buy – formatted or unformatted?
6 How much did she pay altogether?

4 Types of disks

Look at the illustrations and find out:

1 the two standard disk sizes (dimensions) used with PCs
2 the meaning of the abbreviations 'DS', 'DD' and 'HD'
3 the storage capacities of double density and high density disks (5.25 inch and 3.5 inch)
4 the external features of double density and high density disks
5 the storage capacity of the floppy disk that is made of barium ferrite.

Check your answers with a partner.

5.25-inch diameter disk (used in old computers)
Small, flexible magnetic disk supplied within a plastic envelope.
Options:
a 360 KB, double density
b 1.2 MB, high density

3.5-inch micro-floppy disk, DS, DD
Double-sided, double density. 720/800 KB capacity. Conventional disk with ferrous (iron) oxide surface

3.5-inch floppy disk 2HD
Double-sided, high density. 1.44 MB capacity.
Conventional disk

3.5-inch microdisk
Extended density. 2.88 MB capacity.
Recording material: barium ferrite

5 Reading

A   Read the text and look at the diagrams.

Technical details

Information stored in the RAM is lost when the computer is turned off. Because of this, data and applications are stored in either hard or floppy disks which provide a more permanent backing store.

Floppy disks are so called because they consist of flexible plastic material which has a magnetizable surface. They are available in two sizes: 5.25-inch disks are used in old computers, 3.5-inch disks are the most popular today.

The surface of a floppy disk is divided into concentric circles or 'tracks', which are then divided into 'sectors'. When you insert a blank disk into a disk drive, it must be 'initialized', or formatted, before information can be recorded onto it. This means that magnetic areas are created for each track and sector, along with a catalogue or 'directory' which will record the specific location of files.

When you save a file, the operating system moves the read/write heads of the disk drive towards empty sectors, records the data and writes an entry for the directory. Later on, when you open that file, the operating system looks for its entry in the directory on the disk, moves the read/write heads to the correct sectors, and reads the file into the RAM area.

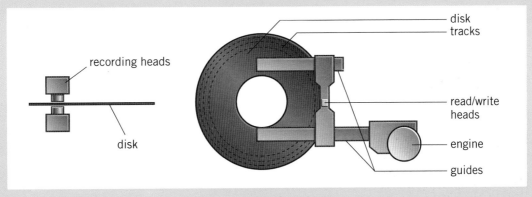

Disk drive: the electronic mechanism that accepts,
reads and writes data on a disk

Match the words and expressions on the left with the explanations on the right.

1 backing store	a a catalogue of where each piece of data is stored and how to find it
2 floppies	b recording heads
3 disk drive	c secondary storage
4 formatting	d diskettes
5 directory	e initializing; setting tracks and sectors on magnetic disks
6 read/write heads	f a peripheral which spins disks and contains a read/write head

**B Look at the illustration.
Identify some tracks and sectors.**

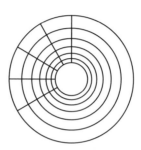

6 Word building

A From the noun *magnet* we can form other words:

> 1 magnetic   2 magnetically   3 magnetism   4 magnetize
> 5 magnetizable   6 magnetized   7 magnetizing

Decide which part of speech each word is. Then use the correct words to complete these sentences.

8 .... is the science of magnetic phenomena and properties.
9 Floppy and hard disks are considered as .... storage devices.
10 Information is recorded on a disk in the form of .... spots called bits.

B From the verb *record* (pronounced /rɪˈkɔːd/) we can build up other words:

> recorder   recording   recorded

Complete these sentences with the correct words.

1 All disks must be initialized before information can be .... onto them.
2 The .... heads follow the tracks and magnetize the coating along each track.
3 A disk drive works very much like a tape .... that can both play and record.

Unit 12 *Hard drives*

1 Before you read

Try to answer these questions.

1 What is the main function of a hard disk?
2 Which unit is used to measure hard disk capacity?
3 Can you think of one advantage that hard disks have over floppies?

A hard disk spins at about 7,200 revolutions per minute – 20 times the speed of a floppy disk drive

2 Reading

A **Read the text quickly to find out if you were right in Task 1.**

B **Read the text again and make a list of the technical aspects that you should consider when buying a hard disk.**

When buying a hard disk ...

Hard disks have important advantages over floppy disks: they spin at a higher speed, so you can store and retrieve information much faster than with floppies. They can also hold
5 vast amounts of information, from 500 MB up to several gigabytes. Apart from this, both types of disks work in the same way. To directly access the necessary information, the read/write heads of rigid disks seek the
10 required tracks and sectors, and then transfer the information to the main memory of the computer or to another form of storage, all of which is done in a few milliseconds (ms).

Bearing in mind that you always need disk
15 storage, it is good sense to ask yourself some vital questions: What size capacity do I need? What speed can I use? What kind of storage device is the most suitable for my

requirements? If you only use word-processing programs, you will need less storage capacity 20 than if you use CAD, sound and animation programs. For most users, 2 GB on the hard disk is enough.

Now let's turn our attention to speed. Access times vary from 8 ms to 20 ms. 'Access time' – 25 or seek time – is the time it takes your read/write heads to find any particular record. You have to distinguish clearly between seek time (e.g. 20 ms) and 'data transfer rate' (the average speed required to transmit data from a 30 disk system to the RAM, e.g. at 20 megabits per second). Remember that the transfer rate also depends on the power of your computer.

When buying a hard disk you should consider the kinds of drive mechanisms and products 35 available. There are 'internal' and 'external' drives which are both fixed hard drives, i.e. rigid disks sealed into the drive unit, either within or attached to the computer. A third type of hard drive, known as 'removable', allows information to be recorded on 'cartridges', which can be removed and stored off-line for security purposes. Popular removable hard disks include Jaz and Zip drives. A Jaz cartridge can store up to 2 GB of data, whereas a Zip drive can store up to 250 MB of data.

Finally, a few words about 'optical' technology: CD-ROMS and CD-Recordable drives have become a reality. However, magnetic hard disks are still preferred for personal data storage, whereas optical discs are used for recording large amounts of information such as a dictionary or encyclopedia.

40

45

50

HELP box

- **ms**: milliseconds (thousandths of a second)

- **CAD**: computer-aided design

- **CD-ROM**: acronym for Compact Disk – Read Only Memory

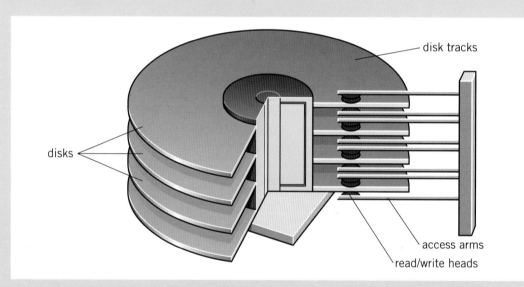

A hard disk can hold large amounts of information because it uses multiple disks, or platters, stacked on top of one another.

C   Now read these sentences and decide if they are true (T) or false (F).

1   Hard disks use rigid rotating disks.   ☐
2   'Seek time' refers to the average time required for the recording heads to move and access data.   ☐
3   If you use multimedia applications, you need the same storage capacity as required for word processors.   ☐
4   'Access time' and 'data transfer rate' mean the same.   ☐
5   Optical disks are magnetic.   ☐
6   Each Jaz cartridge can hold up to 1,000 MB of data.   ☐
7   CD-ROM disks are used for storage of massive amounts of information.   ☐

Check your answers with another student.

3 Vocabulary

The phrase *hard disk* consists of the adjective *hard* and the noun *disk*. Make other phrases or words by combining *hard* and *disk* with these words. Give the meaning of each phrase or word in your own language. (Use your dictionary if necessary.)

copy sell drive

drugs

worker

optical

internal   hard | disk   magnetic

compact   labour

currency   capacity

ware   directory

time

4 Listening

Look at the diagrams and try to answer the questions. Then listen to Vicky Cameron, an IT lecturer, and check your answers.

1 Which is more efficient: a new hard disk or one that has been used for a few months?
2 How does a hard disk store information, if possible? In contiguous or non-contiguous sectors?
3 How does fragmentation affect a computer's performance?
4 How does a defragmenting program help restore a fragmented disk?

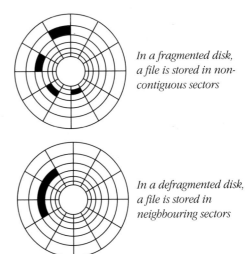

In a fragmented disk, a file is stored in non-contiguous sectors

In a defragmented disk, a file is stored in neighbouring sectors

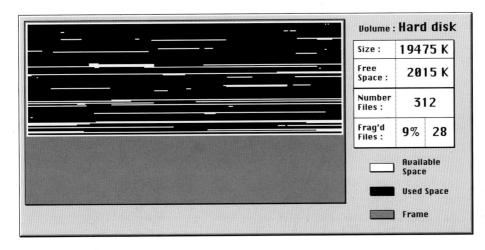

Volume :	**Hard disk**	
Size :	**19475 K**	
Free Space :	**2015 K**	
Number Files :	**312**	
Frag'd Files :	**9%**	**28**

☐ Available Space
■ Used Space
▨ Frame

A typical fragmented disk: the free space is spread all over the drive

5 Follow-up: A hard disk advertisement

Complete the advertisement for the MegaMind hard disk with the words in the box.

megabytes	drive	compatible	highest	time
protection	secure	write	multimedia	

MegaMind X T

Today's personal computers are very powerful, but to handle large applications like databases, (1) .... , DTP publishing and CAD, you need to have more than 200 (2) .... in your hard disk. That's where MegaMind XT comes in: a reliable hard (3) .... with 6 gigabytes of capacity; 8 ms average seek (4) .... and 13 mbits/sec average data transfer rate; and a 3.5" drive unit with a five-year warranty.

You also receive software utilities that let you easily manage and (5) .... your data. Our software provides formatting, partitions, disk optimization and password (6) ....

MegaMind XT is (7) .... with IBM PCs as well as Macintosh computers. As with every MegaMind product — hard disk or optical, 1 GB to 6 GB — the XT gives you the (8) .... performance. So call us today on (0181) 796 0402. Or (9) .... to MegaMind, PO Box 673, London, N22 1XB.

Unit 13 *Optical breakthrough*

1 Warm-up

Before listening try to answer these questions.

1 What is this a picture of?
2 What kind of technology is used by CD-ROM disks and drives?
3 What does 'CD-ROM' stand for?
4 How do you say these expressions in your language?
   compact disk   CD-ROM disk drive
   laser technology   erasable optical disk

2 Listening

Paul (see Unit 5) is now interested in CD-ROMs. He has gone back to his local computer shop to ask for some information.

Read the sentences below, and as you listen put a cross (✗) next to those which contain a technical mistake. Then listen again and correct these sentences.

1 A CD-ROM disk is very different from a compact music disk. ☐
2 You need a hard disk drive to read CD-ROM disks. ☐
3 The data on a CD-ROM is read with a laser beam. ☐
4 A typical CD-ROM disk can hold 100 MB. ☐
5 The data on a CD-ROM can be changed or 'written' to. ☐
6 A CD-ROM is a good way of storing large amounts of
   information (images, sounds, applications, etc.). ☐
7 CD-ROM drives cannot play audio CDs. ☐

A CD-ROM

3 Reading

A   **What are the advantages and disadvantages of optical disks? Read the text to check your answer.**

Optical disks and drives

Optical disks can store information at much higher densities than magnetic disks. Thus, they are ideal for multimedia applications where images, animation and sound occupy a
5 lot of disk space. Besides, they are not affected by magnetic fields. This means that they are secure and stable, e.g. they can be transported through airport metal detectors without damaging the data. However, optical drives are slower than hard drives. While there are hard 10

59

drives with an average access time of 8 ms, most CD-ROM drives have an access time of 150 to 200 ms.

There are various types of optical drives:

15 ● **CD-ROM** systems offer everything, from shareware programs to dictionaries and encyclopedias, from multimedia databases to 3-D games. A lot of institutions have discovered that CD-ROM is the most

20 economical way of sharing information. In fact, one CD-ROM disk (650 MB) can replace 300,000 pages of text (about 500 floppies), which represents a lot of savings in distributing materials and corporate

25 databases. In addition, CD-ROM drives can play music CDs while you work. Yet CD-ROM technology has one disadvantage: you cannot write anything onto a CD-ROM disk. You can only 'read' it, like a book.

30 ● CD-Recorders come in two different forms: **CD-R** and **CD-RW**. CD-R machines record on CD-R (write-once) disks, allowing you to create and duplicate CDs. They are used to back up hard disks or to distribute and

35 archive information. In fact, these systems are the modern version of old WORM (write once, read many) disks. CD-RW machines hold CD-RW (rewritable) disks that you can erase and re-use, just as you would do with a

40 hard disk.

● The future of optical storage is called **DVD** (digital versatile disk). A DVD-ROM can hold 17 GB, about 25 times an ordinary CD-ROM. For this reason, it can store a large amount of multimedia software and complete 45 Hollywood movies in different languages. They can also play music CDs and CD-ROMs. However, DVD-ROMs are 'read-only' devices. To avoid this limitation, companies also produce DVD rewritable drives. 50

● **Magneto-optical (MO) drives** use both a laser and an electromagnet to record information. Consequently, MO disks are rewritable, i.e. they can be written to, erased, and then written again. They usually come in 55 two formats: (i) 5.25" cartridges can hold more than 2 GB; (ii) 3.5" floptical disks have a capacity of 230 to 640 MB. They are ideal for back-up and portable mass storage.

A DVD drive

B **Read the text again and summarize in the table the most relevant information.**

	Technical specifications	*Use*
CD-ROM		
CD-Recorder		
DVD		
Magneto-optical		

4 Discourse cohesion

Reference signals

A   **Read these sentences and clauses and look back at the text in Task 3 to find out what the words in bold refer to.**

1   ... **they** are secure and stable ... (line 6)
2   ... **which** represents a lot of savings in distributing materials. (line 23)
3   ... **you** cannot write anything onto a CD-ROM disk. (line 27)
4   You can only 'read' **it** ... (line 29)
5   ... CD-RW (rewritable) disks **that** you can erase and re-use ... (line 38)

Connectors and modifiers

B   **Look at the expressions in *italics* in these sentences and clauses.**

1   *Thus*, they are ideal for multimedia applications ...
2   *Besides*, they are not affected by magnetic fields.
3   *However*, optical drives are slower than hard drives.
4   *In addition*, CD-ROM drives can play music CDs while you work.
5   *Yet* CD-ROM technology has one disadvantage: ...
6   *For this reason*, it can store a large amount of multimedia software ...

Put each expression (1 to 6) into the right category: a, b or c.

a   to show contrast
b   to explain causes and results
c   to add new ideas

5 Speaking

Which of the products in the box on page 62 would be most suitable for the purposes below? Discuss the pros and cons with a partner.

1   To store data and programs at home.
2   To hold large amounts of information in a big company.
3   To store an illustrated encyclopedia for children.
4   To hold historical records in the National Library.
5   To store high-quality audio and video, and hold several movies in different languages.

Useful expressions

For personal use, I would recommend ... because ...   *I agree/disagree with you. CD-ROMs ...*

In a big company, it would be a good idea to ...   *Besides, ...*

However, ... is good for an encyclopedia because ...   *Well, that depends on ...*

Products available

Hard disk drive
Superfast 8 ms hard drive. Capacity ranges from 2 to 6 GB.

Iomega's removable drives
The Zip series uses 100 MB and 250 MB disks. In the near future it could replace the floppy disk as the portable storage medium.
The Jaz series can hold 2 GB cartridges. Ideal to back up hard disks.

CD-ROM drive
Each CD disk holds 650 MB.

CD-Recordable drive
Makes it possible to write data to CDs as well as read it.

Magneto-optical (MO) disk systems
Erasable optical-magnetic 5.25" cartridges with 2.6 GB of storage capacity. Can be erased and written on like a hard disk.
Rewritable 3.5" floptical disks with a storage capacity of 640 MB.

DAT Data tape drive
Digital audio tape drives to store computer data. Used for back-up purposes. Slow access. Huge amounts of information (about 10 GB).

Digital Video Disk-ROM drive
Each DVD-ROM disk has a capacity of up to 17 GB, and can hold various full-screen movies. The drive can also read your CD-ROMs.

Students using CD-ROMs

6 Crossword

Read the clues and complete the crossword.

Across

1 Acronym for 'light amplification by stimulated emission of radiation'. (5)

4 A microcomputer. (2)

6 To write information on a disk, magnetic tape or film. (6)

10 To record and keep for future use. (5)

12 Abbreviation of 'binary digit'. (3)

14 Thousandth of a second. (11)

15 The type of computer with a 286 processor introduced by IBM in 1984. (2)

17 Concentric ring marked on the surface of a disk when the disk is formatted. (5)

18 Prefix meaning 'very large' or 'one thousand million'. (4)

20 Read only memory. (3)

22 The physical mechanism that accepts, reads and writes data on a disk. (5)

Down

1 Acronym for 'local area network'. (3)

2 Opposite of 'indelible'. (8)

3 Abbreviation of 'high density' or 'hard disk'. (2)

5 Way of storing a lot of information in a removable form. (9)

7 Abbreviation of 'optical character recognition'. (3)

8 All disks must be 'initialized' or .... when used for the first time. (9)

9 Indelible optical storage device: 'write once, read many'. (4)

11 Not cheap. (9)

13 A flat, circular surface used to hold computer data. (4)

16 Opposite of 'soft'. (4)

19 Disk that holds music. (2)

21 A thousand kilobytes. (2)

Basic software

Learning objectives

In this section you will learn how to:

- extract relevant information from texts about system software
- recognize the characteristics of a typical graphical user interface or GUI
- make a summary of a written text
- talk about word processors
- identify the function of different word-processing capabilities: search and replace, cut and paste, spell checkers, etc.
- understand the basic features of spreadsheets and databases
- acquire specific vocabulary related to Internet utilities.

Unit 14 *Operating systems*

1 Warm-up

A **Look at the diagram. What is the function of the operating system?**

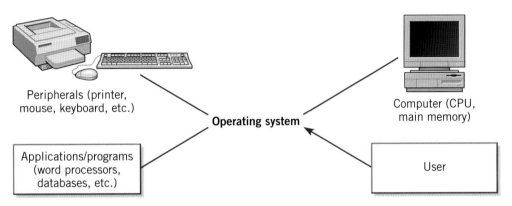

Peripherals (printer, mouse, keyboard, etc.)

Operating system

Computer (CPU, main memory)

Applications/programs (word processors, databases, etc.)

User

B **Read the text below and complete it with the phrases in the box.**

applications software   operating system   software   system software

Information provided by programs and data is known as (1) ....
Programs are sets of instructions that make the computer execute operations and
tasks. There are two main types of software:

● The (2) .... refers to all the programs which control the basic
functions of a computer. They include operating systems, system utilities
(e.g. an anti-virus program, a back-up utility) and language translators
(e.g. a compiler – the software that translates instructions into machine code).

● The (3) .... refers to all those applications – such as word
processors and spreadsheets – which are used for specific purposes.
Applications are usually stored on disks loaded into the RAM memory
when activated by the user.

The (4) .... is the most important type of system software. It is
usually supplied by the manufacturers and comprises a set of programs and files
that control the hardware and software resources of a computer system. It
controls all the elements that the user sees, and it communicates directly with
the computer. In most configurations, the OS is automatically loaded into the
RAM section when the computer is started up.

2 Reading

Read the text and find:

1 the text-based operating system delivered with most PCs
2 the mail package included with Windows '98
3 the function of the Finder in Macintosh computers
4 the meaning of 'multitasking'
5 the operating system which is written in C language and has been adopted by many corporate installations as standard
6 the OS that is freely redistributable under the GNU general public licence
7 the OS used by Digital computers
8 the OS created to run Java applications.

Operating systems

MS-DOS	This is the disk operating system developed in 1981 by Microsoft Corp. It is the standard OS for all IBM PC compatibles or clones. In this text-based operating system, you communicate with the computer by typing commands that exist within its library. For example, some basic DOS commands include DIR (shows a list of all the files in a directory), COPY (makes a duplicate of a file), DEL (deletes files).
Windows '95/'98 	**Windows '95** is a bootable operating system in its own right. It has a graphical interface with many Macintosh-like features. It supports multimedia applications and comes with Internet software. The program manager is called Windows Explorer. Buttons and scroll-bars have an attractive, three-dimensional look. With **Windows '98**, Internet access becomes part of the user interface. Its active desktop lets you find information easily with the same view of content on your PC, network or the Web. The system includes Outlook Express for e-mail, NetMeeting conferencing software, a chat program and a Web-page editor. It offers support for new technologies like DVD and it also enables you to watch TV on your PC.
Windows 2000	This OS is an update to all Windows versions, including Windows NT.
Macintosh (Apple)	Most of the Mac OS code is in the ROM chips. These contain hundred of routines (sequences of instructions) which perform such tasks as starting up the computer, transferring data from disks to peripherals and controlling the RAM space. Large parts of the Mac OS are also inside the System file and the Finder, kept in the System folder. The content of the System file is loaded automatically at start-up, and contains information which modifies the routines of the OS in the ROM chips. The Finder displays the Macintosh's desktop and enables the user to work with disks, programs and files. It allows multitasking. It has an Internet set-up assistant, an e-mail program and a Web browser.

OS/2 Warp (IBM) 	This is the PC world's most technically sophisticated operating system. It provides true multitasking, allowing a program to be divided into 'threads', many of which can be run at the same time. Thus, not only can numerous programs run simultaneously, but one program can perform numerous tasks at the same time. The IBM OS/2 Warp includes easy access to networks via modem, support for Java applications and voice recognition technology.
UNIX	This operating system, designed by Bell Laboratories in the USA for minicomputers, has been widely adopted by many corporate installations. From the very first, it was designed to be a multitasking system. It is written in C language. It has become an operating environment for software development, available for any type of machine, from IBM PS/2s to Macs to Cray supercomputers. UNIX is the most commonly used system for advanced CAD programs.
Linux (Linus Torvalds)	Protected under the GNU general public license, Linux is the open source, cooperatively-developed POSIX-based, multitasking operating system. Linux is used as a high value, fully-functional UNIX® workstation for applications ranging from Internet Servers to reliable work group computing. Linux is available for Intel®, Alpha™ and Sun SPARC® platforms.
Open VMS	The Open VMS operating system is Digital's popular general purpose OS for all VAX computers. It provides data and access security. Open VMS supports all types of Digital and multivendor networks.
JavaOS (JavaSoft)	This is designed to execute Java programs on Web-based PCs. It's written in Java, a programming language that allows Web pages to display animation, play music, etc. The central component of JavaOS is known as the Java Virtual Machine.

3 Basic DOS commands

Match the DOS commands on the left with the explanations on the right. Some commands are abbreviations of English words.

1	FORMAT	a erases files and programs from your disk
2	CD (or CHDIR)	b copies all files from one floppy disk to another
3	DIR	c changes your current directory
4	MD (or MKDIR)	d initializes a floppy disk and prepares it for use
5	DISKCOPY	e displays a list of the files of a disk or directory
6	BACKUP	f changes names of your files
7	REN (or RENAME)	g creates a subdirectory
8	DEL	h saves the contents of the hard disk on floppy disks for security purposes

4 Listening

A 🔊 **Read the information in the box and then listen to four advertisements from a radio programme about computers.**

> **System utilities** are small programs which improve a system's performance and help users take advantage of the computer's capabilities. They are often desk accessories that can be called up while you're working in another application. They can also be INITs, i.e. system extensions which are activated when you turn on the computer, control devices which you adjust in the control panel, or even stand-alone programs that run when you need them. Utilities are available for back-up, file search, virus protection, disaster recovery, and so on.

Number these system utilities in the order in which you hear them.

☐ screen saver
☐ virus detector
☐ crashed disk rescuer and data recovery
☐ printing aid

B 🔊 **Listen again. Which utility would you use for each of these requirements?**

1 To work on one document while another is printing. ....
2 To diagnose and repair damaged disks. ....
3 To automatically blank out the screen after a specific interval of inactive time (so that the image does not burn into the screen). ....
4 To protect your system against computer viruses. ....

5 Quiz

**Work with a partner. Try to answer as many questions as possible.
(Use the Glossary if you need to.)**

1 What name is given to the set of programs that interface between the user, the applications programs and the computer?
2 What type of programs are designed for particular situations and specific purposes?
3 What does 'MS-DOS' stand for?
4 What is the basic DOS command for copying a file?
5 The Macintosh operating system is kept in various locations. Where exactly are these?
6 Can you give a synonym for the term 'routine'?
7 What is the abbreviation for 'International Business Machines'?
8 Which company developed UNIX?
9 Which programming language allows you to play animations on the Web?
10 What are the effects of computer viruses?

Unit 15 *The graphical user interface*

1 A user-friendly interface

The picture below illustrates a user interface based on graphics.

Read the definitions in the HELP box and then find the following interface elements in the picture:

1 window boxes
2 scroll bars
3 menu bar
4 pull-down menu
5 pointer
6 icons
  a documents
  b applications
  c wastebasket (*trash* in American English)
  d disks: hard, floppy, removable, CD-ROM
  e printer
  f folders

HELP box

- **window:** a viewing area less than or equal to the screen size. By using different windows you can work on several documents or applications simultaneously

- **pull-down menu:** a menu that the user 'pulls down' from a name in the menu bar at the top of the screen by selecting the name with the mouse

- **the pointer:** an arrow, controlled by the mouse, that allows you to move around the screen or to scroll up and down through the document or to give commands

- **icons:** graphic images (or intuitive symbols) used to represent an object or task

- **folders:** containers for documents and applications, similar to the subdirectories of a PC platform

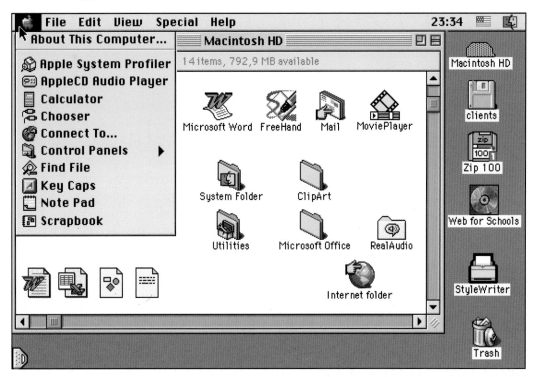

The interface elements of the Macintosh

2 Reading

A **Read the article below and decide which of the expressions in the box best describe a graphical user interface (GUI).**

user-friendly	slow	attractive	text-based	complex	graphics-based

GUIs

The term **user interface** refers to the standard procedures the user follows to interact with a particular computer. A few years ago, the way in which users had access to a computer system was quite complex. They had to memorize and type a lot of commands just to see the content of a disk, to copy files or to respond to a single prompt. In fact, only experts used computers, so there was no need for a user-friendly interface. Now, however, computers are used by all kinds of people and as a result there is a growing emphasis on the user interface.

A good user interface is important because when you buy a program you want to use it easily. Moreover, a graphical user interface saves a lot of time: you don't need to memorize commands in order to execute an application; you only have to point and click so that its content appears on the screen.

Macintosh computers – with a user interface based on graphics and intuitive tools – were designed with a single clear aim: to facilitate interaction with the computer. Their interface is called WIMP: **Window**, **Icon**, **Mouse** and **Pointer** (see p. 69) and software products for the Macintosh have been designed to take full advantage of its features using this interface. In addition, the ROM chips of a Macintosh contain libraries that provide program developers with routines for generating windows, dialog boxes, icons and pop-up menus. This ensures the creation of applications with a high level of consistency.

Today, the most innovative GUIs are the Macintosh, Microsoft Windows and IBM OS/2 Warp. These three platforms include similar features: a desktop with icons, windows and folders, a printer selector, a file finder, a control panel and various desk accessories. Double-clicking a folder opens a window which contains programs, documents or further nested folders. At any time within a folder, you can launch the desired program or document by double-clicking the icon, or you can drag it to another location.

The three platforms differ in other areas such as device installation, network connectivity or compatibility with application programs.

These interfaces have been so successful because they are extremely easy to use. It is well known that computers running under an attractive interface stimulate users to be more creative and produce high quality results, which has a major impact on the general public.

B **Look at the text again and guess the meaning of these words in your own language.**

1 user interface (line 1)   2 commands (line 6)   3 tools (line 21)
4 program developer (line 30)   5 platform (line 36)
6 desktop (line 37)   7 file finder (line 38)   8 nested folders (line 42)

C Find answers to these questions.

1 What does the abbreviation 'GUI' stand for?
2 What is the contribution of Macintosh computers to the development of graphic environments?
3 What does the acronym 'WIMP' mean?
4 What computing environments based on graphics are mentioned in the text?
5 How do you run a program on a computer with a graphical interface?
6 Can you give two reasons for the importance of user-friendly interfaces?

3 Listening

Listen to this radio interview with Bill Thompson, a program developer. He is talking about Microsoft Windows operating systems. Complete this fact file.

Publisher	Main features	The Windows family	What you need to use Windows	Windows applications (examples)
Microsoft Corp.	(1) .... interface, friendlier than (2) .... Dynamic Data Exchange: 'hot links' (connections) between common data in different programs.	(3) .... for desktop PCs and portables. (4) .... for high-performance workstations and file servers on networks. They'll be replaced by Windows 2000.	Processor: (5) .... RAM memory: (6) .... 4 GB hard disk VGA compatible monitor	(7) .... for Windows. Lotus 1-2-3 for Windows.

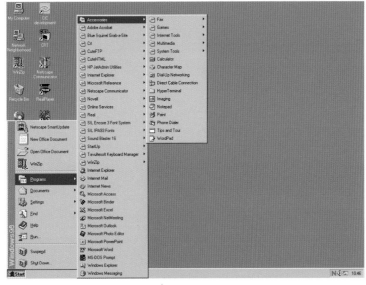

A sample screen from Windows '98's desktop

4 Writing

Summarize the text in Task 2 in 70–75 words. You may like to follow these steps.

1   Read through the whole text again and think of a suitable title for it.
2   Make sure you understand all the main points. Go through the text and **underline** the relevant information in each paragraph.
3   **Make notes** about the main points:
    ● omit repetitions and unnecessary phrases
    ● leave out details, such as examples.
    E.g. notes on the first paragraph: *In the past only experts used computers. But now, emphasis on user-friendly interfaces.*
4   **Make sentences** from the notes and connect the sentences by using **linking** words (*and, but, also, because, that's why, in fact, therefore,* etc.). Write your **first draft**.
5   Improve your first draft by **reducing sentences** (see HELP box below).
6   Check grammar, spelling and punctuation. Write the **final version** of your summary.

HELP box
Ways of reducing sentences

● Transform a relative clause into an *-ing* participle clause
  e.g. *Icons are graphic images that represent tasks ...*
  = *Icons are graphic images **representing** tasks.*

● Take out relative pronouns where possible
  e.g. *The software (that) we bought last year ...*

● Omit qualifying words (adjectives or modifying adverbs)
  e.g. *(quite) complex/(very) similar*

● Take out *that* in reported speech or thought
  e.g. *It is well known (that) computers ...*
  I think (that) there's something wrong with this program.

● Cut out unnecessary phrases
  e.g. *Macintosh computers were designed with a clear aim: to facilitate the user's interaction with the computer.*
  = *Macintosh machines were designed to facilitate the user's interaction with the computer.*

Unit 16 *A walk through word processing*

1 Before you read

Try to answer these questions.

1 What is a word processor?
2 What makes word processors superior to traditional typewriters?
3 Make a list of the most important features offered by word processors.

2 Reading

A **Read the text on page 74 and underline any word-processing capabilities that you did not list in Task 1.**

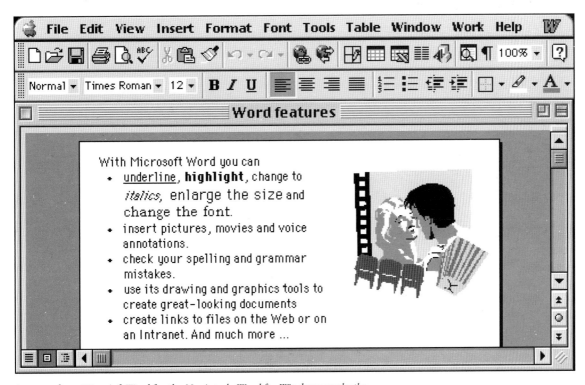

A screen from Microsoft Word for the Macintosh. Word for Windows works the same way. WordPerfect, AmiPro and WordStar also have multiple typefaces, windows, pull-down menus and other graphical tools

Word-processing facilities

Writing letters, memos or reports are the ways most people use computers. They manipulate words and text on a screen – primarily to print at some later time and store for safe keeping. Computers alleviate much of the tedium associated with typing, proofing and manipulating words. Because computers can store and recall information so readily, documents need not be retyped from scratch just to make corrections or changes. The real strength of word processing lies in this ability to store, retrieve and change information. Typing is still necessary (at least, for now) to put the information into the computer initially, but once in, the need to retype only applies to new information.

Word processing is more than just typing, however. Features such as **Search** and **Replace** allow users to find a particular phrase or word no matter where it is in a body of text. This becomes more useful as the amount of text grows.

Word processors usually include different ways to view the text. Some include a view that displays the text with editor's marks that show hidden characters or commands (spaces, returns, paragraph endings, applied styles, etc.). Many word processors include the ability to show exactly how the text will appear on paper when printed. This is called WYSIWYG (What You See Is What You Get, pronounced 'wizzy-wig'). WYSIWYG shows **bold**, *italic*, underline and other type style characteristics on the screen so that the user can clearly see what he or she is typing. Another feature is the correct display of different typefaces and **format** characteristics (margins, indents, super- and sub-scripted characters, etc.). This allows the user to plan the document more accurately and reduces the frustration of printing something that doesn't look right.

Many word processors now have so many features that they approach the capabilities of **layout applications** for desktop publishing. They can import graphics, format multiple columns of text, run text around graphics, etc.

Two important features offered by word processors are automatic **hyphenation** and **mail merging**. Automatic **hyphenation** is the splitting of a word between two lines so that the text will fit better on the page. The word processor constantly monitors words typed and when it reaches the end of a line, if a word is too long to fit, it checks that word in a hyphenation dictionary. This dictionary contains a list of words with the preferred places to split it. If one of these cases fits part of the word at the end of the line, the word processor splits the word, adds a hyphen at the end and places the rest on the next line. This happens extremely fast and gives text a more polished and professional look.

Mail merge applications are largely responsible for the explosion of 'personalized' mail. Form letters with designated spaces for names and addresses are stored as documents with links to lists of names and addresses of potential buyers or clients. By designating what information goes into which blank space, a computer can process a huge amount of correspondence substituting the 'personal' information into a form letter. The final document appears to be typed specifically to the person addressed.

Many word processors can also generate tables of numbers or figures, sophisticated indexes and comprehensive tables of contents.

(Adapted from *Understanding Computers*, N. Shedroff *et al.* Sybex, 1993)

B **Look at the words in the box and complete the following sentences with them. Use the information in the text or Glossary if necessary.**

> type style   WYSIWYG   format   indent
> font menu   justification   mail merging

1 .... stands for 'What you see is what you get'. It means that your printout will precisely match what you see on the screen.

2 .... refers to the process by which the space between the words in a line is divided evenly to make the text flush with both left and right margins.

3 You can change font by selecting the font name and point size from the ....

4 .... refers to a distinguishing visual characteristic of a typeface; 'italic', for example is a .... that may be used with a number of typefaces.

5 The .... menu of a word processor allows you to set margins, page numbers, spaces between columns and paragraph justifications.

6 .... enables you to combine two files, one containing names and addresses and the other containing a standard letter.

7 An .... is the distance between the beginning of a line and the left margin, or the end of a line and the right margin. Indented text is usually narrower than text without ....

C **Match the words and expressions on the left with their explanations on the right.**

1 retrieve
2 typefaces
3 header
4 footer
5 subscripted character
6 hyphenation

a text printed in the top margin
b recover information from a computer system
c letter, number or symbol that appears below the baseline of the row of type; commonly used in maths formulas
d text printed in the bottom margin
e division of words into syllables by a short dash or hyphen
f styles for a set of characters; sometimes called 'fonts'

3 Listening

Two friends are talking about how to move text by using the 'Cut and Paste' technique. Read the conversation and complete it with words from the box.

> finally   command   first   Edit
> now   mistake   next   insertion

A: Do you know how I can move this paragraph? I want to put it at the end of this page.

B: Er ... I think so. (1) .... you use the mouse to select the text that you want to move ... and then you choose the Cut (2) .... from the Edit menu ...

A: Like this?

B: Yes. The selected text disappears and goes onto the Clipboard. And (3) .... you find where you want the text to appear and you click to position the (4) .... point in this place.

A: Mm ... is that OK?

B: Yes, if that's where you want it. (5) .... choose Paste from the (6) .... menu, or hold down Command and press V. (7) .... check that the text has appeared in the right place.

A: What do I do if I make a (8) .... ?

B: You can choose Undo from the Edit menu which will reverse your last editing command.

A: Brilliant! Thanks a lot.

B: That's OK.

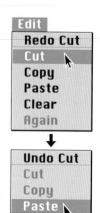

💿 **Now listen to check your answers.**

4 Writing

Moving text is a process of cutting and pasting, as if you were using scissors and glue. The picture below represents this process. Write a short description of it.

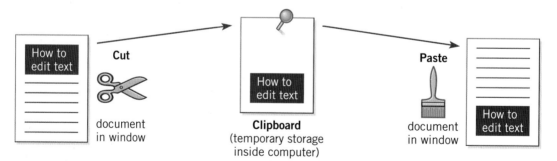

document in window   **Clipboard** (temporary storage inside computer)   document in window

5 Writing tools

A   **Three major features that word processors offer are spell checkers, online thesauruses and grammar checkers. Read the descriptions of these features and match them with the windows or dialog boxes.**

1 **Spell checkers** can be used to compare words in the program's dictionary to those used in the user's document. The spell checker points out any words it cannot match, notifies the user and allows them to make any changes; it sometimes even suggests possible correct spellings.

Replace : file — Replace | original
With : file ▼ — Look up | Cancel
Meanings for : file   Synonyms :
filing system (noun)   Repository
computer item (noun)   card file
metal tool (noun)   register
rank (noun)
put on file (noun)
apply (noun)
scrape with a file (v)

a

Like a conventional thesaurus, this database of words contains definitions and suggestions of words with similar and opposite meanings. A word may be spelled correctly but still be wrong (*too* instead of *two*, for instance). This is a good first step at proofing a document because it can find many common errors, but users will still need to proofread documents to ensure complete accuracy.

2 Many word processors include an **online thesaurus** with which users can look up different words to use in similar instances. Their power comes not from knowing every grammatical rule, but from questioning the writer about certain parts of the text. Some even include information about pronunciation and histories of evolving meaning.

Sentence :   Ignore
A grammar checker **are** an application   Change
that attemps to check grammatical...   Next Sentence
                                    Ignore Rule
Suggestions :   Close
Consider **is** instead of **are**   Explain...
                                    Options...

b

3 **Grammar checkers** are applications that attempt to check more than just spelling. They count words in sentences to flag possible run-on sentences. They look for words that show possible conflicts

Not in Dictionary : hiphenate
Change to : hyphenate   Ignore | Ignore all
Suggestions : hyphenate   Change | Change all
                           Add | Close
                           Suggest | Options...
Add words to Custom diction ▼

c

between verbs and subjects and they offer advice about corrections. Grammar checkers are a step beyond spell checkers, but they are still not a substitute for a human editor. However, this does not mean that all of the words in the document are spelled correctly. This gives the writer another chance to think about what he or she has written; the computer can alert writers to problems that wouldn't be obvious to them otherwise.

(Texts adapted from *Understanding Computers*, by N. Shedroff *et al.* Sybex, 1993)

B **Read through the descriptions again. There are three sentences which have been printed in the wrong position. Decide which are the intruding sentences and where they should go.**

6 Speaking

Work in pairs. Read the table below which summarizes the most relevant features of two word-processing programs. The characteristics of each program are marked with a tick (✓). Student A has *Printext* and Student B has *Publisher*. Explain to your partner why your program is better.

Example

A: With Printext I can …

B: Yes, but you can't …

A: However, it is possible to … whereas with Publisher you can't …

B: Yes, but don't forget that with Publisher you can … Moreover, …

A: OK. I understand what you mean, but what about …?

Characteristics	Student A Printext	Student B Publisher
1 Instantaneous WYSIWYG and editing	✓	✓
2 Variety of font types, styles and size	✓	✓
3 Editing facilities: Copy, Cut, Paste, Undo, Select All	✓	✓
4 Centring and indenting paragraphs. Special column formats. Hyphenation and justification of text with optimum line-breaking	✓	✓
5 Spell checker, grammar checker and thesaurus	✓	✓
6 Can find and replace words even in unopened files	✓	
7 Automatic numbering of chapters and sections. Automatic generation of indexes and tables of contents. Cross-reference facilities		✓
8 Allows you to generate maths formulas, and diagrams		✓
9 Graphics tools: You can have the text wrap around the graphic or flow through it. You can scale and rotate graphics	✓	
10 Import and export facilities. You can transfer files to other IBM PCs and Macintosh applications	✓	
11 You can record voice annotations to insert comments into a document		✓
12 Includes Internet connection tools and allows you to create HTML pages for the Web		✓

Unit 17 *Spreadsheets*

1 Looking at a spreadsheet

Look at this spreadsheet and try to answer the questions.

1 What is a spreadsheet? What is it used for?

2 In a spreadsheet, there are 'columns', 'rows' and 'cells'. Give an example of each from the sample spreadsheet.

3 What type of information can be keyed into a cell?

4 What will happen if you change the value of a cell?

	A	B	C	D	E
1		1997	1998		
2	Sales	$890	$982		
3	Stocks/Shares	487	760		
4	Interest	182	324		
5	Total Revenue	1559	2066		
6					
7	Payroll	894	904		
8	Publicity	399	451		
9	Services	438	372		
10	Total Expenses	1731	1727		
11					
12	TOTAL	-172	339		
13					
14					

This sample spreadsheet shows the income and expenses of a company. Amounts are given in $millions

2 Listening

A 📀 **Listen to Lucy Boyd, a software developer, talking about spreadsheet programs and the spreadsheet above and check your answers to Task 1.**

B 📀 **Listen again and decide whether these sentences are right (✓) or wrong (✗).**

1 A spreadsheet program displays information in the form of a table, with a lot of columns and rows. ☐

2 In a spreadsheet you can only enter numbers and formulas. ☐

3 In a spreadsheet you cannot change the width of the columns. ☐

4 Spreadsheet programs can produce visual representations in the form of pie charts. ☐

5 Spreadsheets cannot be used as databases. ☐

C **Look at the spreadsheet in Task 1 again and mark the boxes with a ✓ or an ✗. Then check your answers with another student.**

6 The value of the cell C12 is the result of applying the formula 'C5 – C10'. ☐

7 The cell B5 is the result of adding the values in cells B2 and B3. ☐

8 If you type the value '800' in C3, the values in cells C5 and C12 will be recalculated. ☐

3 Vocabulary

Match the terms in the box with the explanations below.

a formula   b cell   c sales   d payroll   e share(s)   f revenue
g interest   h expenses

1 A sum of money that is charged or paid as a percentage of a larger sum of money which has been borrowed or invested, e.g. *High ~ rates./7 per cent ~ on a loan.* ☐

2 The intersection of a column and a row in a spreadsheet, e.g. *the ~ B2.* ☐

3 The quantity sold, e.g. *The ~ of PCs rose by 10 per cent last year.* ☐

4 The income – or money – received by a company or organization, e.g. *The annual ~ of this multinational company is …* ☐

5 A ~ in a company is one of the equal parts into which the capital of the company is divided, entitling the holder of the ~ to a proportion of the benefits, e.g. *£10 ~s are now worth £11.* ☐

6 Financial costs; amounts of money spent, e.g. *Travelling ~.* ☐

7 A function or operation that produces a new value as the result of adding, subtracting, multiplying or dividing existing values, e.g. *If we enter the ~ B5–B10, the program calculates …* ☐

8 **1** A list of people to be paid and the amount due to each. **2** Wages or salaries paid to employees, e.g. *He was on the company's ~.* ☐

4 Graphic representation

A **Look at the graph on page 81 and, with the help of a partner, check that it is an exact visual representation of the spreadsheet in Task 1.**

B **Can you calculate the net profits of this firm during the period 1997–98?**

C **What type of image is this: a pie chart, a bar chart, an area graph or a line graph?**

D What is the advantage, if any, of displaying information as a graph, rather than as a spreadsheet?

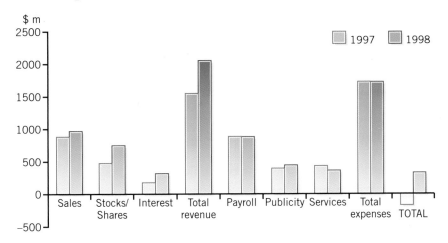

5 Extension

A Spreadsheet programs are also used to make out invoices. Look at the invoice below and fill in the blanks with the right words from the box.

Quantity	Description	Price	VAT (Value Added Tax)
Reference	TOTAL	Address	Company

Name:	Redwood Comprehensive School			Invoice

Springbank Road, Easthill

Telephone: 436171   **Date:** 12 May 1999

				Total
Ulysses Classic	64 MB of RAM, 9 GB HD	12	£ 1,050	£ 12,600
XGA Monitor	Colour 16"	9	225	2,025
Video Card	Millions of colours	5	316	1,580
Portable Ulysses	32 MB RAM, 2 GB HD	3	1,190	3,570
Laser SAT	PostScript	1	825	825
Scanner JUP	Flatbed. Includes OCR	2	675	1,350
		Subtotal	£ 21,950
		17.5%	3,841
			£ 25,791

Ulysses Computers, Inc.

B Have you got a spreadsheet program at work or school? If so, try to produce a similar invoice.

Unit 18 *Databases*

1 Warm-up

Companies often use databases to store information about customers, suppliers and their own personnel. Study the illustrations and then try to answer these questions.

1 What is a database?
2 Which tasks can be performed by using a database? Make a list of possible applications.
3 What do the terms mean in your language: **file**, **record**, **field**?

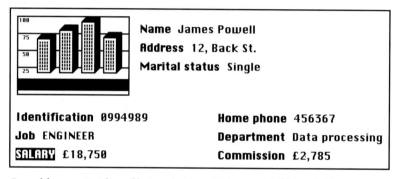

Name James Powell

Address 12, Back St.

Marital status Single

Identification 0994989

Job ENGINEER

SALARY £18,750

Home phone 456367

Department Data processing

Commission £2,785

Record from an Employee file in a database. This record holds ten fields (the illustration is one)

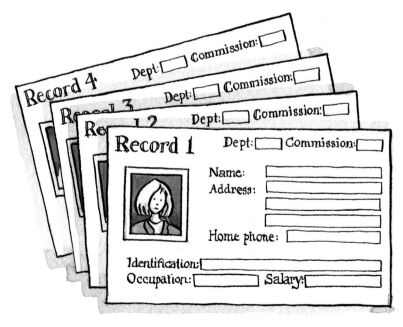

Record 4   Dept: ☐ Commission: ☐

Record 3   Dept: ☐ Commission: ☐

Record 2   Dept: ☐ Commission: ☐

Record 1   Dept: ☐ Commission: ☐

Name: ☐
Address: ☐
☐
☐

Home phone: ☐

Identification: ☐
Occupation: ☐   Salary: ☐

A database file stores information in fields grouped on records

2 Reading

A   **Here is part of an article about databases. First, read all the way through and underline the basic features of a database.**

Basic features of database programs

With a **database** you can store, organize and retrieve a large collection of related information on computer. If you like, it is the electronic equivalent of an indexed filing cabinet. Let us look at some features and applications.

- Information is entered on a database via **fields**. Each field holds a separate piece of information, and the fields are collected together into **records**. For example, a record about an employee might consist of several fields which give their name, address, telephone number, age, salary and length of employment with the company. Records are grouped together into **files** which hold large amounts of information. Files can easily be updated: you can always change fields, add new records or delete old ones. With the right database software, you are able to keep track of stock, sales, market trends, orders, invoices and many more details that can make your company successful.

- Another feature of database programs is that you can automatically look up and find records containing particular information. You can also search on more than one field at a time. For example, if a managing director wanted to know all the customers that spend more than £7,000 per month, the program would search on the name field and the money field simultaneously.

A computer database is much faster to consult and update than a card index system. It occupies a lot less space, and records can be automatically sorted into numerical or alphabetical order using any field.

The best packages also include networking facilities, which add a new dimension of productivity to businesses. For example, managers of different departments can have direct access to a common database, which represents an enormous advantage. Thanks to security devices, you can share part of your files on a network and control who sees the information. Most aspects of the program can be protected by user-defined passwords. For example, if you wanted to share an employee's personal details, but not their commission, you could protect the commission field.

In short, a database manager helps you control the data you have at home, in the library or in your business.

B   **Now make a list of the words you don't understand. Can you guess their meaning? Compare your ideas with other students.**

C   **Using the information in the text, complete these statements.**

1   A database is used to ....
2   Information is entered on a database via ....
3   Each field holds ....
4   'Updating' a file means ....
5   The advantages of a database program over a manual filing system are

    ....
6   Access to a common database can be protected by using ....

3 Puzzle

Complete the sentences by using a term from the list. Then write the words in the crossword to find the hidden message.

database	field	layout	merging	record	sorted	updated

1 In order to personalize a standard letter you can use 'mail ....' (a technique which consists of combining a database with a document made with a word processor).

2 Records can be automatically .... into any order.

3 You can decide how many fields you want to have on a ....

4 Files can easily be .... by adding new information or deleting the old one.

5 A .... program can be used to store, organize and retrieve information of any kind.

6 The .... of the records can be designed by the user.

7 Each piece of information is given in a separate ....

4 Language work: Plurals

A **Look at the HELP box and then write the plural of these words:**

1 slot   5 fax
2 key   6 mouse
3 directory   7 floppy
4 businessman   8 virus

B **Look at the text again and find five plurals pronounced /ɪz/.**

HELP box
Plurals

- In most cases, the plural in English is written with an 's'.
  record → records
  – The plural is written with 'es' after 's', 'sh', 'x' or 'ch'.
  address → addresses   box → boxes
  – With nouns which end in a consonant + 'y', the 'y' becomes 'i' and 'es' is added.
  technology → technologies
  – But if the 'y' follows a vowel, only 's' is added.
  day → days

- **Special plural forms**
  man → men
  child → children
  analysis → analyses
  formula → formulae/formulas

- Pronunciation of the 's'.
  – /s/ after one of the sounds /p/, /t/, /k/, /f/ or /θ/
  chips, amounts
  – /ɪz/ after one of the sounds /s/, /z/, /ʃ/, /tʃ/ or /dʒ/
  processes, cartridges
  – /z/ in most other cases
  drives, customers, files

C 📀 **Put these plurals in the correct pronunciation column. Then listen and check your answers.**

passwords	laptops	budgets	images	fields	taxes
graphics	expenses	folders	interfaces	disks	pixels

/s/	/ɪz/	/z/

5 Listening

A 📀 **Listen to Helena Davies, an IT trainer, explaining how to use mail merging to some employees. Number these steps in the order that you hear them.**

☐ Activate the Mail Merge command (Print Merge in some programs). This combines the main document and the data document.

☐ Click 'Print' and the program generates a single letter for each record in the data document.

☐ Create the data document with a database program or with the right spreadsheet software. This document contains rows with names, addresses and other information that will be merged with the standard letter.

☐ Create the main document with a word processor. Type the standard letter and insert the appropriate field names into it.

B **Look at the illustration of mail merging and identify the three types of documents involved in this example of mail merging.**

	A	B	C	D	E	F
1	Title	First name	Last name	Street	City	Postcode
2	Mr	Fred	Jones	15 The Calls	Leeds	LS2 6JU
3	Mrs	Diana	Read	18 Union Street	Glasgow	G1 3TA
4	Ms	Carol	Taylor	75 Windmill Street	London	W1P 1HH
5	Mr	Jack	Gordon	7 Piccadilly Street	York	YO1 1PN

The data document contains the fields and the information that is different in each version of the letter

《DATA Mailing》
《Title》《First Name》《Last name》
《Street》
《City》《Postcode》

Dear 《Title》《Last name》,
We are pleased to inform you that an updated version of Top Project is now available. To obtain your copy, simply call us and we'll send you, absolutely free, the new version of the program.

We also enclose a catalogue with the new range of SunRise machines and the latest software products. There are special offers for all our clients, including a book about budgeting and balancing. To order by phone, call 01332 8430477.

Yours sincerely,

Barry Stephens
Sales Manager
Sunrise Computers
19 Park Avenue
Derby

The main document contains the standard letter

Mr Fred Jones
15 The Calls
Leeds LS2 6JU

Dear Mr Jones,
We are pleased to in
an updated version of
now available. To obt
simply call us and w
absolutely free, the n
the program.

We also enclose a c
the new range of Sun
and the latest softw
There are special off
clients, including a
budgeting and balan
by phone, call 01332

Yours sincerely,

Barry Stephens
Sales Manager
Sunrise Computers
19 Park Avenue
Derby

Mrs Diana Read
18 Union Street
Glasgow G1 3TA

Dear Mrs Read,
We are pleased to info
an updated version of T
now available. To obtai
simply call us and we
absolutely free, the ne
the program.

We also enclose a cat
the new range of SunRi
and the latest softwa
There are special offer
clients, including a
budgeting and balanci
by phone, call 01332 84

Yours sincerely,

Barry Stephens
Sales Manager
Sunrise Computers
19 Park Avenue
Derby

Ms Carol Taylor
75 Windmill Street
London W1P 1HH

Dear Ms Taylor,
We are pleased to infor
an updated version of To
now available. To obtain
simply call us and we'll
absolutely free, the new
the program.

We also enclose a cata
the new range of SunRise
and the latest software
There are special offers
clients, including a b
budgeting and balancing
by phone, call 01332 843

Yours sincerely,

Barry Stephens
Sales Manager
Sunrise Computers
19 Park Avenue
Derby

Mr Jack Gordon
7 Piccadilly Street
York YO1 1PN

Dear Mr Gordon,
We are pleased to inform you that an updated version of Top Project is now available. To obtain your copy, simply call us and we'll send you, absolutely free, the new version of the program.

We also enclose a catalogue with the new range of SunRise machines and the latest software products. There are special offers for all our clients, including a book about budgeting and balancing. To order by phone, call 01332 8430477.

Yours sincerely,

Barry Stephens
Sales Manager
Sunrise Computers
19 Park Avenue
Derby

Merging the main document and the data document generates personalized versions of the letter

6 Writing

Imagine that you are Barry Stephens, the sales manager of Sunrise Computers. Write a standard letter to your clients about 'New software products on the market' and offer them a free demonstration disk.

Unit 19 *Faces of the Internet*

1 Get ready for listening

Try to answer these questions.

1 What is the Internet?
2 What can you do on the Internet?
   Make a list of possible applications.

A program like Microsoft Internet Explorer allows you to search, view and manage information over the Web.
http://www.microsoft.com/ie/

2 Listening

🔊 **Peter Morgan, the director of Text Link, is talking to a journalist about the Internet. Listen and complete the journalist's notes.**

- To connect to the Internet you need:
  (1) .... (2) .... (3) ....
- One cable of the modem is connected to the (4) .... of your computer and the other to the (5) ....
- To get your Internet identity you need to have an account with a (6) ...., a company that offers connection for an annual fee.
- Services offered by the Internet: (7) .... (10) ....
                                      (8) .... (11) ....
                                      (9) ....
- The Web is a huge collection of (12) .... stored on computers all over the world.

3 Reading

A **Which Internet utility (1 to 7) would you use to do each of these tasks (a to g)? Read the text on page 88 to check your answers.**

1 e-mail
2 Web browser
3 Newsreader
4 IRC/chat program
5 FTP software
6 Videoconferencing
7 Telnet

a send a message to another person via the Internet
b transfer files from the Internet to your hard disk
c have a live conversation (usually typed) on the Internet
d connect to a remote computer by entering certain instructions and run programs on it
e take part in public discussion areas, called newsgroups
f fetch and view Web pages on the Internet
g participate in live conversations, using text, audio and video

Internet software

Getting connected

The language used for data transfer on the Internet is known as TCP/IP (transmission control protocol/Internet protocol). This is like the Internet operating system.

5

The first program you need is a PPP (point to point protocol) driver. This piece of software allows the TCP/IP system to work with your modem; it dials up your Internet service provider (ISP), transmits your password and log-in name and allows Internet programs to operate.

10

E-mail

E-mail is your personal connection to the Internet. It allows you to exchange messages with people all over the world. It can include text, pictures, and even audio and animation.

15

When you set up an account with an ISP, you are given a unique address and anyone can send you e-mail. The mail you receive is stored on the server of your ISP until you next connect and download it to your hard disk.

20

Web browsers

The Web is a hypertext-based system where you can find news, pictures, games, online shopping, virtual museums, electronic magazines – any topic you can imagine.

25

You navigate through the Web using a program called a 'browser', which allows you to search and print Web pages. You can also click on keywords or buttons that take you to other destinations on the net. This is possible because browsers understand hypertext markup language (HTML), a set of commands that indicate how a Web page is formatted and displayed.

30

IRC, audio and video chatting

IRC – Internet relay chat – is a system for real-time (usually typed) conversation. It's easy to use. To start a chat session you run an IRC program, which connects you to an IRC server – a computer dedicated to IRC. Then you join a channel, which connects you to a single chat

35

40

area. Next you type a message and the other participants can see it.

Internet telephone and video chatting are based on IRC protocols. Videoconferencing programs enable users to talk to and see each other, and collaborate. They are used in intranets – company networks that use Internet software but make their Web site accessible only to employees and authorized users.

45

50

FTP and Telnet

With **FTP** software you can copy programs, games, images and sounds from the hard disk of a remote computer to your hard disk. Today this utility is built into Web browsers.

55

A **Telnet** program is used to log directly into remote computer systems. This enables you to run programs kept on them and edit files directly.

Newsgroups

Newsgroups are the public discussion areas which make up a system called 'Usenet'. The contents of the newsgroups are contributed by people who send articles (messages) or respond to articles. They are classified into categories: *comp* (computers), *misc* (miscellaneous), *news* (news), *rec* (recreation), *soc* (society), *sci* (science), *talk* and *alt* (alternative).

60

65

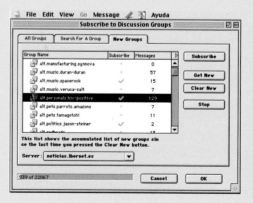

To take part in newsgroups you need to run a
newsreader and subscribe to a certain group

B   **Read the text again and choose the right answer.**

1   An Internet service provider (ISP) is
  a   a program that connects you to the Internet.
  b   a company that gives you access to the Internet.

2   HTML is
  a   the software which allows you to fetch and see Web pages.
  b   the codes used to create hypertext documents for the Web.

3   An IRC channel is
  a   an IRC discussion area.
  b   a computer system dedicated to IRC.

4   Usenet is
  a   a big system of public discussion groups.
  b   a newsgroup.

5   An intranet is
  a   like a small version of the Internet inside a company.
  b   a commercial online service.

4 Speaking

Imagine you are taking part in an IRC session with a friend.
Complete the dialogue. Then act out the conversation.

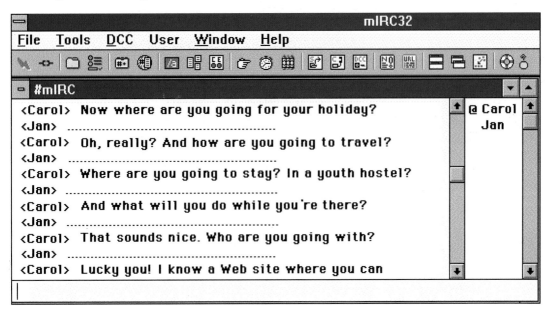

mIRC for Windows is a typical Internet relay chat program.
You can get it at http://www.mirc.co.uk/

5 A typical Web page

A **The picture below illustrates a typical Web page. Look at the HELP box and then find the following features in the picture:**

1 URL address
2 Basic functions of the toolbar:
    a go to the home page
    b retrace your steps
    c go forward one page
    d interrupt the current transfer
    e update a page
    f find words within a page
    g load and display the page's images
3 Clickable image link
4 Clickable hypertext link

HELP box

● **URL:** uniform resource locator, the address of a file on the Internet. A URL looks like this:
http://www.netscape.com/
   – 'http://' means hypertext transfer protocol and tells the program to look for a Web page
   – 'www' means World Wide Web
   – 'netscape.com' is the domain name and tells people that it is a commercial enterprise

● **navigation buttons:** buttons on the toolbar which allow you to go back or forward to other Web pages. You can also return to your start-up page or stop the transfer when the circuits are busy

● **links:** shortcuts (underlined text or images) that, when clicked, take you to other Web pages

● **security on the Web:** just a few Web sites are secure. When the page is not encrypted, the security lock is open

A sample screen from Netscape Communicator, a leading program for work on the Internet.
http://www.netscape.com/

B **Have you ever surfed the Web? What are your favourite Web sites? Tell your partner about it.**

C **Look at these tasks and choose the most suitable Web site from the cyberlist.**

1 Read about environmental problems
2 Get news reports
3 Find out about specific hardware and software
4 Make flight reservations
5 Read about films and Hollywood awards
6 Search for Web addresses

http://www.yahoo.com/
http://www.greenpeace.org/
http://www.ibm.com/
http://www.fly.virgin.com/
http://www.telegraph.co.uk/
http://www.oscars.org/

6 Writing

A **Study the format of the Internet address. Then read the header of the e-mail below and identify the sender, the recipient and the line that describes the content. Is there an attached file? How do you say 'attachment' in your language?**

B **Write a reply to the e-mail message.**

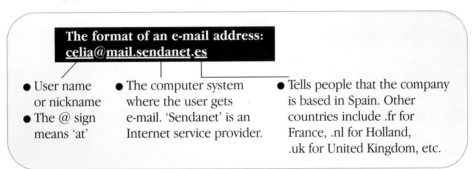

The format of an e-mail address:
celia@mail.sendanet.es

- User name or nickname
- The @ sign means 'at'

- The computer system where the user gets e-mail. 'Sendanet' is an Internet service provider.

- Tells people that the company is based in Spain. Other countries include .fr for France, .nl for Holland, .uk for United Kingdom, etc.

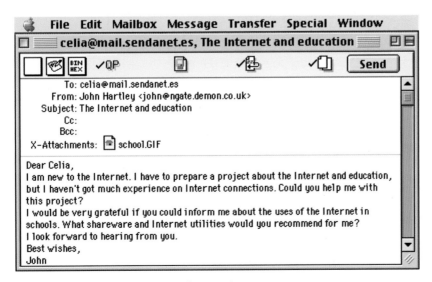

File Edit Mailbox Message Transfer Special Window

celia@mail.sendanet.es, The Internet and education

To: celia@mail.sendanet.es
From: John Hartley <john@ngate.demon.co.uk>
Subject: The Internet and education
Cc:
Bcc:
X-Attachments: school.GIF

Dear Celia,
I am new to the Internet. I have to prepare a project about the Internet and education, but I haven't got much experience on Internet connections. Could you help me with this project?
I would be very grateful if you could inform me about the uses of the Internet in schools. What shareware and Internet utilities would you recommend for me?
I look forward to hearing from you.
Best wishes,
John

A sample screen from Eudora, a popular e-mail program.
Qualcomm's Eudora is available at http://www.eudora.com/

Creative software

Learning objectives

In this section you will learn how to:

- identify the functions of different graphics tools
- understand specific aspects of desktop publishing and multimedia applications
- write a letter to a newspaper asking for information about the hardware and page-layout software used for its production
- build up new words by using prefixes, suffixes and compounds
- acquire the basic vocabulary associated with graphical representations, desktop publishing and multimedia technology.

Unit 20 *Graphics and design*

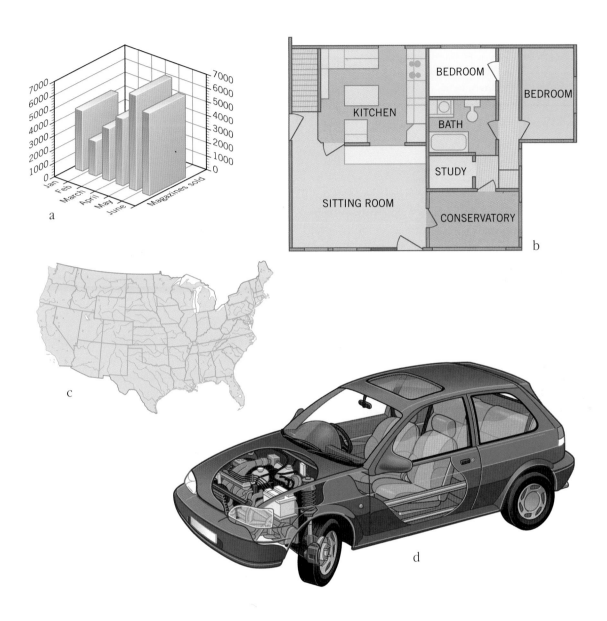

a

b

c

d

1 Warm-up

1 Look at the pictures above, which were all created on computer. Which ones are three-dimensional? What are the advantages of creating three-dimensional images?
2 From the pictures, can you suggest which people might use computer graphics professionally? What would they use them for?
3 Can you think of other professionals who use computer graphics? How do they use them?

2 Reading

Read through the text and find the answers to these questions.

1 What are 'computer graphics'?
2 What do the acronyms 'CAD', 'CAE' and 'CAM' stand for?
3 What are the benefits of using computer graphics in the car industry?
4 What are the benefits of using graphics in business?
5 What is 'computer animation'?

Computer graphics

Computer graphics are pictures and drawings produced by computer. A graphics program interprets the input provided by the user and transforms it into images that can be displayed on the screen, printed on paper or transferred to microfilm. In the process the computer uses hundreds of mathematical formulas to convert the bits of data into precise shapes and colours. Graphics can be developed for a variety of uses including presentations, desktop publishing, illustrations, architectural designs and detailed engineering drawings.

Mechanical engineers use sophisticated programs for applications in computer-aided design and computer-aided manufacturing. Let us take, for example, the car industry. CAD software is used to develop, model and test car designs before the actual parts are made. This can save a lot of time and money.

Computers are also used to present data in a more understandable form: electrical engineers use computer graphics to design circuits and people in business can present information visually to clients in graphs and diagrams. These are much more effective ways of communicating than lists of figures or long explanations.

Today, three-dimensional graphics, along with colour and animation, are essential for such applications as fine art, graphic design, Web-page design, computer-aided engineering and academic research. Computer animation is the process of creating objects and pictures which move across the screen; it is used by scientists and engineers to analyse problems. With the appropriate software they can study the structure of objects and how it is affected by particular changes.

Basically, computer graphics help users to understand complex information quickly by presenting it in a clear visual form.

3 Listening

A ▣◉ **Read the passage below and complete it. Then listen and check your answers.**

A basic tool palette

A graphics (1) p............................. is the software that enables you to draw and manipulate objects on a computer. Each graphics package has its own facilities, plus a wide range of basic drawing and (2) p............................. tools. The collection of tools in a package is known as a palette.

The basic shapes which are used to make (3) g.............................. objects are
called 'primitives'. These are usually geometric, such as lines between two
points, arcs, (4) c.............................. , polygons, ellipses and even text. You can
choose both the primitive you want and where it should go on the screen.
Moreover, you can specify the (5) 'a.............................' of each primitive,
such as its colour, (6) l............................. type, fill area, interior style and so on.

The various tools in a palette usually appear together as pop-up
(7) i.............................. in a menu. To use one you activate it by
(8) c.............................. on it. For example, if you want to draw a rectangle, you
activate the rectangle tool and the pop-up options allow you to choose the
origin of the rectangle (using the insertion point as its centre or corner) and
the possibility of (9) d............................. a rectangle with rounded corners.

B **Look at the functions represented by the icons in the tool palette on the left and
match them with the definitions on the right.**

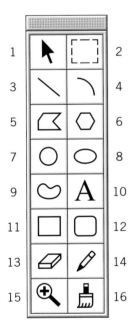

1 2
3 4
5 6
7 8
9 10
11 12
13 14
15 16

a This is used to scale the view. Similar to the command 'Zoom in/out'.
b This is used to delete the part of the picture you drag it over. It is known as 'Eraser'.
c This is used to type text.
d This draws a straight line between two points.
e This is a paintbrush used to add colour and patterns. It often comes in different shapes.
f This is used to draw polygons with irregular sides.
g This is used to draw thin, free-form lines.
h These are used to select text and images.
i This draws an arc, or part of a circle.
j This draws curved, free-form shapes.
k This is used to draw a circle with two foci, known as an ellipse.
l These two are used to draw all kinds of rectangles, even ones with rounded corners.
m This is used to draw a circle.
n This is used to draw polygons with equal sides.

4 More about graphics

A **Graphics programs have several options that work in conjunction with the
tools menu to enable the user to manipulate and change pictures.**

**Look at the facilities on the left and match them with the definitions on
the right.**

1	Patterns menu	a	Turning an image round.
2	Scaling	b	A tool which lets you scale the 'view' of a picture and edit a small portion of it as if you were working under a magnifying glass. It is very useful for doing detailed work as you can edit the picture one dot at a time.
3	Rotating	c	Making the object larger or smaller in any of the horizontal, vertical or depth directions.
4	Inverting	d	A shading technique where two different colours are placed next to each other; the human eye blends the colours to form a third one. It is also used to show shading in black and white.
5	Zoom	e	A palette from which you choose a design to fill in shapes.
6	Slanting	f	Reversing the colour of the dots in the selected part of a picture, so that white dots become black and black dots become white.
7	Black-and-white dithering	g	Inclining an object to an oblique position.

B **Look at the pictures and label them with the facility that has been used to change the original.**

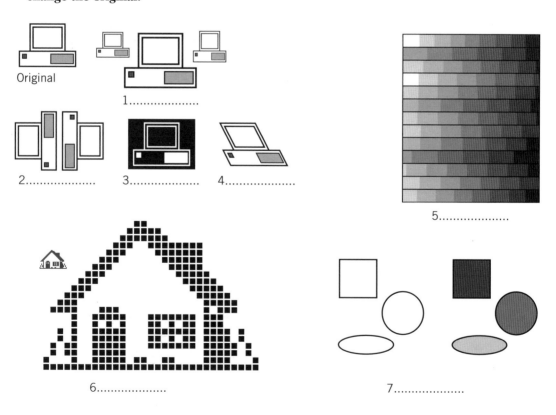

Original

1....................

2.................... 3.................... 4....................

5....................

6.................... 7....................

5 Language work: Gerunds (*-ing* nouns)

A   Read the passage below, then look at the HELP box. Underline the gerunds and
decide whether they function as the subject, the subject complement, the
object of a verb, or the object of a preposition.

You cannot create a picture simply by specifying primitives. Instead, you must specify the primitives and their attributes, then transform them by specifying where and how you want them placed on the screen so they create your picture. Transformation means moving or otherwise manipulating the object by translating, rotating and scaling the object.

Translation is moving an object along an axis to somewhere else in the viewing area. Rotation is turning the object around an axis. Scaling is making the object larger or smaller in any of the horizontal, vertical or depth directions (corresponding to the x, y and z axes). The term rendering describes the techniques used to make your object look real. Rendering includes hidden surface removal, shading, light sources and reflections.

(from *Introduction to Computer Graphics*, ©Hewlett-Packard Limited, 1989)

B   Complete the sentences by using an
appropriate gerund from those in the box.

creating   adding   clicking
processing   printing   rendering

1   Graphic artists like .... colour
    and depth to their drawings and designs.
2   A 32-bit painting program has a complete
    palette of tools for .... images
    from scratch.
3   The speed of a microprocessor is important
    in .... information.
4   Before .... a document, the user
    should decide on the layout.
5   You can open the colour palette by
    .... on the corresponding
    pop-up icon.
6   .... refers to the techniques
    used to make realistic images.

HELP box
Gerunds

Gerunds are nouns formed by adding *-ing* to
verbs. A gerund usually functions as:

*   the subject of a verb, e.g. *Smoking is bad for
    your health*.
*   the object of a verb, e.g. *She has never done
    any computing*.
*   the object of a preposition, e.g. *CAD
    programs are very fast at performing drawing
    functions*.
*   the complement of the subject, e.g. *His
    favourite pastime is playing computer games*.

*Rendering shows differences
in light and shade*

6 Speaking

Work in pairs. **Student A: turn to page 143 and Student B: turn to page 147.**

Work in pairs. **Student A: turn to page 143 and Student B: turn to page 147.**

Unit 21 *Desktop publishing*

1 Warm-up

Look at the illustration below and, with a partner, write down some answers to these questions.

1 What types of files are combined in desktop publishing?
2 What kinds of documents can be produced with desktop publishing software?

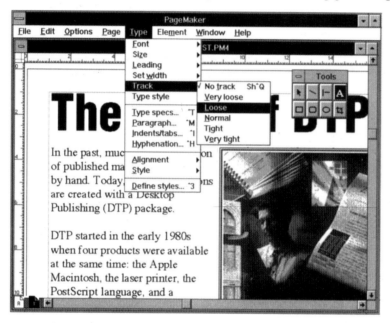

A screen from PageMaker, a leading DTP package. Another program often associated with DTP is QuarkXPress

2 Reading

A **Read the text and check your answers to Task 1.**

What is 'desktop publishing'?

'Desktop publishing' refers to the use of personal computers to design, implement and publish books, newsletters, magazines and other printed pieces. Desktop publishing is really a combination of a few different processes including word processors, graphic design, information design, output and pre- press technologies, and sometimes image manipulation. There are also many applications that support these processes, including font creation applications (that allow users to design and create their own typefaces, called fonts) and type manipulation applications (that allow users to modify text in visually creative ways).

Desktop publishing centres around a **layout application**. A layout application is used to import text from word processing applications, graphics from paint and drawing applications and images from scanning or image manipulation applications, and to combine and arrange them all on a page. They typically can bring in or import many different types of files. It is this ability to manipulate so many different items and control how they are used that makes layout software so popular and useful. This software is usually the last stop before a document is printed. Once composed and designed, these files can be printed onto film by high quality devices, called **imagesetters**, and printed on a traditional printing press.

Because imagesetters are expensive devices, most people cannot afford to buy their own. There are, however, companies called **service bureaux** that specialize in printing other people's files on imagesetters, just like copy stores make copiers available to others. Service bureaux can offer imageset output, laser printer output, colour laser printer output and even slide or film recorder output. In addition, some have colour scanning equipment.

(Adapted from *Understanding Computers*, N. Shedroff *et al.* Sybex, 1993)

B   Read the text again and complete these sentences.

1   A page layout application can import and combine ....
2   Font creation software enables users to ....
3   Imagesetters are used to ....
4   Service bureaux offer services such as ....

3 Word building

Look at the HELP box which lists ways of forming new words in English. Then in pairs, look at these words and decide:

● **which process of word formation has been applied**

● **what part of speech each word is**

● **where the stress falls in each word. Underline the stressed syllable(s).**

1	upgrade	9	manipulation
2	imprint	10	publishing
3	printed	11	publisher
4	print-out	12	newsletter
5	interactive	13	visually
6	printing press	14	typeface
7	pre-press	15	professional
8	creative	16	imagesetter

HELP box
Word formation

New words are formed in three main ways in English:

1 Affixation
  ● adding a prefix to the base:
    print → reprint
  ● adding a suffix to the base:
    print → printer
2 Conversion, i.e. assigning one class to another:
    print v → *print* n
3 Compounding, i.e. adding one base to another:
    finger + print → fingerprint

4 Listening

📢 **Listen to this radio interview with Ros Jackson about the importance of fonts and typography in desktop publishing and choose the correct answer.**

1 What does Ms Jackson do?
   a She's an advertiser.
   b She's a font software designer.
   c She's a DTP professional.

2 Fonts refer to
   a the style of a typeface.
   b the size of a typeface.
   c the style and size of a typeface, for example

   Helvetica italic in 12 point.

3 According to Ms Jackson, fonts and other type characteristics
   a don't make any difference to a message.
   b are important in order to communicate a message clearly and make it look attractive.
   c help designers scale and rotate type and text.

4 Scalable fonts are stored as
   a a whole image made up of dots, which cannot be changed.
   b an outline which can be changed.

5 PostScript fonts were created by
   a Apple and Microsoft.
   b Bitstream.
   c Adobe Systems.

Bookman at 12pt	**Chicago** at 12pt
Courier	**Chicago by night**
Σψμβολ (Symbol)	**Blackoak**
✤✱■✳✿❈▼▲ (Zapf Dingbats)	Old Dreadful no.7
	Orbit-B
Palatino	PIONEER
Helvetica Italic	SHOTGUN
Times Bold Italic	DIGITAL
Zapf Chancery	

Some different fonts

5 Computers for newspapers

A   The letter below is from a group of students asking for information about the hardware and publishing software used by the newspaper *El Independiente*.

Read it and note:
- the form and position of the addresses
- the polite forms of asking for cooperation:
  - *We would be very grateful if you could …*
  - *Could you also …*
- the ways in which the letter begins and ends.

B   Work in pairs. Student A: turn to page 144 and Student B: turn to page 148.

C   Write a letter to the *Morning News* asking for information about the hardware and page-layout software used in its production. Use the letter on the right to help you.

Rhondda
Comprehensive School

31 Prospect Place, Treorchy, Wales

The Editor   28th October 1998
El Independiente
c/ Moratin, 7
28006 Madrid
Spain

Dear Sir/Madam

We are writing to ask if you can help us with our school project. We are doing a survey of the major newspapers in the European Union to find out which computer systems and desktop publishing programs they use.

We would be very grateful if you could tell us which hardware and software you use at *El Independiente*. Could you also tell us whether you have a Web edition published on the Internet? Thank you very much.

We look forward to hearing from you.

Yours faithfully,

Katherine Powell
Katherine Powell
Student representative

Your address
....
....
....

Date.............................

The Editor
Morning News
14 Pennington Street
London EC1 6XJ

Unit 22 *Multimedia*

1 Multimedia is here!

Look at the cover for Encarta '99.
What types of data are integrated
in multimedia applications?

2 Listening

A ▱◉ A sales assistant is explaining the components of a multimedia system to
a customer. Listen and complete this diagram.

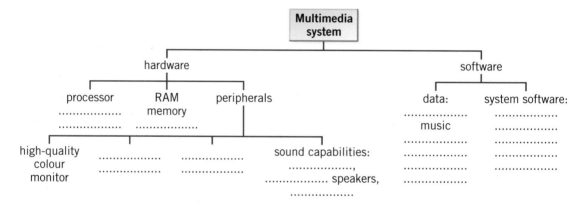

Compare your answers with another student.

B ▱◉ Now listen again and answer these questions.

1 What is multimedia?
2 What is the advantage of computer multimedia presentations over TV and video?
3 Which system software is designed by Apple for multimedia work?
   a Windows with Multimedia control panels
   b QuickTime
4 Can an existing PC be adapted for multimedia applications?

3 Reading

A Read the texts and match them with the headings in the box below.

Sound, Music, MIDI   CD-ROM titles full of pictures, action and sound!
CD-ROM is more than just heavy metal   The potential of using multimedia

Multimedia magic!

1 ....

Until now multimedia applications have been used mainly in the fields of information, training and entertainment. For example, some museums, banks and estate agents have information kiosks that use multimedia. Several companies produce training programmes on optical disks, and marketing managers use presentation packages (like Microsoft PowerPoint or Lotus Freelance Graphics for Windows) to make business presentations. They have all found that moving images, sound and music involve viewers emotionally as well as inform them, and make their message more memorable.

2 ....

Sound is an important component of the multimedia approach. The effective use of sound can be used to grab the attention of the participant, set the mood or underscore a point. The most popular way of delivering sound is the hardware sound board. Such boards offer two important capabilities. The first of these is a built-in stereo synthesizer complete with a built-in audio amplifier. Just connect a set of speakers and

Musicians can compose, mix and edit music electronically by connecting a computer to special MIDI instruments

you've got instant sound, music and speech capabilities. The second capability is the musical instrument digital interface, or MIDI. This is a specialized serial interface that allows an electronic musical instrument to communicate with other MIDI-equipped instruments or PCs.

3 ....

Between 80 and 90 per cent of all multimedia applications are distributed on CD-ROM, some just on CD, some on several media (as with Autodesk's Multimedia Explorer, which comes with both a CD-ROM and diskettes). The reasons for CD-ROM's popularity in multimedia is simple – a single CD can contain 650 MB of data. That's over 500 floppy disks' worth of programs, sound and graphics. The newest CD-ROM standard, CD-ROM XA (for eXtended Architecture) uses data compression to fit even more on these shiny discs. Many XA drives are also compatible with Kodak's PhotoCD technology, that digitizes photographs and places them on a CD-ROM.

4 ....

Electronic encyclopedias integrate text, pictures and sound, and usually have a video section with a full motion video window. *The Compton's Encyclopedia* enables you to read about whales, look at photos of whales, listen to whale songs and view an animated sequence showing whale movements through the ocean. Similarly, the *Grolier Encyclopedia* lets you read about birds, view pictures of birds, and listen to recordings of their songs.

Other CD-ROMs include dictionaries, guides and courses about history, science, the human body, cinema, literature, foreign languages, etc. For example, *Cinemania* from Microsoft has information on thousands of films and photographs, reviews, biographies and dialogues from films.

(Sections 2 and 3 adapted from 'Upgrading to multimedia' in *PC Upgrade*, June 1993)

B **Read the texts again and correct these statements. There is a technical mistake in each of them.**

1 Multimedia applications do not use huge amounts of data.
2 You don't need to have a sound board on your PC to hear speech and music.
3 Most multimedia software is distributed on magnetic disks.
4 Kodak's PhotoCD technology is not compatible with many CD-ROM drives.
5 There are no language courses available on CD-ROM.

C **Match these terms in the box with the explanations.**

> a Computer animation   b Video computing   c MIDI interface
> d CD-ROM player   e Multimedia control panels

1 Small programs inside the OS designed to work with audio and video files. ☐
2 A code for the exchange of information between PCs and musical instruments. ☐
3 A drive used to handle CD-ROM disks. ☐
4 Manipulating and showing moving images recorded with a video camera or captured from a TV or video recorder. ☐
5 Images which move on the screen. ☐

4 Language work: *If*-clauses

A **Look at the HELP box and then read these sentences. Identify the tenses used in the *if*-clause and in the main clause.**

1 If you upgrade your PC, you'll be able to run multimedia applications.
2 If the marketing manager had a multimedia system, she could make more effective presentations.

B **Put the verbs in brackets into the correct form.**

1 If I (get) .... a sound card, I'll be able to create my own music with a MIDI.
2 If the system (have) .... a SuperVGA card, we would obtain a better resolution.
3 You won't be able to play CD-ROM disks if you (not have) .... a CD-ROM drive.
4 If you (come) .... to the annual computer exhibition, you could see the new Macs.
5 If I could afford it, I (buy) .... a Multimedia PC.

HELP box
Conditional clauses

When you want to talk about a possible situation and its consequences, you use a conditional sentence. Here we examine two types of conditionals:

● First conditional (possible situation)
If A happens ‾ B will happen.
(present simple) (*will* + verb)
e.g. *If you **click** on the speaker icon, you'll **get** a piece of dialogue from the movie.*
In the main clause we can also have a modal (*can*), an imperative, or a present tense verb.

● Second conditional (unlikely situation)
If A happened   B would happen.
(past simple)   (*would* + verb)
e.g. *If I **had** the money, I **would** (I'd) **invest** in a multimedia upgrade kit.*
Other modals (*could, should, might*) may appear in the main clause.

5 Multimedia on the Web

A **Read the text and find:**

1 the function of the extension that is usually added to a file name
2 the language used to create the majority of text files on the Web
3 the graphics interchange format created by CompuServe to compress images
4 the small program (plug-in) that lets you hear audio recordings on the net
5 the most popular video formats
6 the format created by the Moving Picture Experts' Group to capture, store and play back movies
7 the extension for the files that can be decompressed with a program like *Winzip*.

Recognizing file formats

Web pages can contain different multimedia elements: text, graphics, sounds, video and animation. To identify the format or type of file, an extension (a three-letter suffix) is usually added to the file name when it's saved on disk.

Text

The most common text extensions are **.txt, .pdf, .doc** and **.htm** (or **.html**). Most of the text files that you find on the Web have the extension .htm, created with the hypertext markup language.

Graphics

Graphics on the Web can include pictures, photos, paintings, image-maps and buttons. The most common formats are **.gif** (a standard image format developed by CompuServe) and **.jpg** or **.jpeg** (created by the Joint Photographic Experts' Group).

Sounds

The Internet is a great place to find and hear hit songs, movie soundtracks and recorded interviews. The most common formats are these:

- **.wav**: wave files can be played with Sound Recorder included with Windows
- **.ra** or **.ram**: files generated by RealAudio, a plug-in you can download from the Web.

Video and animation

You can see cartoons and movie clips on the Web, but you need the appropriate software. Video files are usually stored in: **.avi**, **.mov** and **.mpg** (or **.mpeg**) formats. To view MPEG videos you just need Video for Windows. However, to create high-quality movie clips you need a dedicated MPEG expansion card. You can also find animation and 3-D worlds. The two standard tools to manipulate animated worlds are VRML and Java. To view a virtual animation you need a program like QuickTime VR.

Compressed files

When you download files, they're probably compressed. Windows files have a **.zip** extension. Macintosh files usually have a **.sit** extension and are opened with *StuffIt*.

B Look at the illustrations and the texts below. Then, if you have a Web page editor, try to create your own home page.

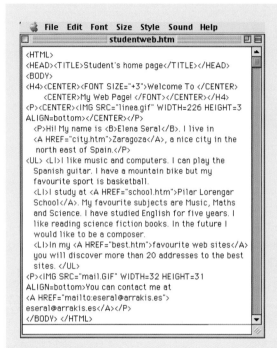

HTML source code

You can create a basic Web page using a text editor (e.g. Windows WordPad or SimpleText), but you need to know the HTML language. HTML commands are called tags and allow you to define text size and font, format paragraphs, add colour and insert links.

HTML file displayed as a Web page

If you don't know the HTML language, you can use a Web page editor (like Abode PageMill, Microsoft FrontPage or Netscape Composer) to simplify the process. These HTML editors automatically produce the tags for text, tables, image maps and frames.

6 Listening

Look at the list of software products and number the items in the order in which you hear them described.

- [ ] Graphics and design
- [ ] Multimedia application
- [ ] DTP
- [ ] Database program
- [ ] Integrated package
- [ ] Educational software
- [ ] Musical software

Programming

Learning objectives

In this section you will learn how to:

- understand basic concepts in programming, and acquire vocabulary connected with it
- recognize acronyms and abbreviations associated with programming
- ask and answer questions about computer languages
- discuss the professional skills and personal qualities required for the jobs of senior programmer and DTP operator
- write a letter applying for a job.

Unit 23 *Program design*

1 Warm-up

A In pairs, try to think of an answer for the question:

What is programming?

Look at the definition in the Glossary. Is it similar to yours?

B Complete the following definitions with the words and phrases in the box.

> the various parts of the program   may occur in programs   language
> binary numbers   a given problem

1 **algorithm**
   The step-by-step specification of how to reach the solution to ....
2 **flowchart**
   A diagram representing the logical sequence between ....
3 **coding**
   The translation of the logical steps into a programming ....
4 **machine code**
   The basic instructions understood by computers. The processor operates on codes which consist of ....
5 **debugging**
   The techniques of detecting, diagnosing and correcting errors (or 'bugs') which
   ....

2 Listening

A 📀 Listen to Lucy Boyd, a software developer, explaining how a program is produced. Number these steps in the order you hear them.

☐ Provide documentation of the program.
☐ Understand the problem and plan the solution.
☐ Test and correct the program.
☐ Make a flowchart of the program.
☐ Write the instructions in coded form and compile the program.

B 📀 Listen again and take notes. Use your notes to explain what each step means.

3 Reading

Read the text and find answers to these questions.

1 Do computers understand human languages?
2 What are the differences between low-level and high-level languages?
3 What is an assembler?
4 What is the function of compilers?
5 What do you understand by the terms **source program** and **object program**?
6 In the future, could computers be programmed in Spanish, French or Japanese?

Programming languages

Unfortunately, computers cannot understand ordinary spoken English or any other natural language. The only language they can understand directly is called **machine code**. This consists of the 1s and 0s (binary codes) that are processed by the CPU.

However, machine code as a means of communication is very difficult to write. For this reason, we use symbolic languages that are easier to understand. Then, by using a special program, these languages can be translated into machine code. For example, the so-called **assembly languages** use abbreviations such as ADD, SUB, MPY to represent instructions. These mnemonic codes are like labels easily associated with the items to which they refer.

Basic languages, where the program is similar to the machine code version, are known as **low-level languages**. In these languages, each instruction is equivalent to a single machine code instruction, and the program is converted into machine code by a special program called an **assembler**. These languages are still quite complex and restricted to particular machines.

To make the programs easier to write and to overcome the problem of intercommunication between different types of machines, higher-level languages were designed such as BASIC, COBOL, FORTRAN or Pascal. These are all problem-oriented rather than machine-oriented. Programs written in one of these languages (known as **source programs**) are converted into a lower-level language by means of a **compiler** (generating the **object program**). On compilation, each statement in a **high-level language** is generally translated into many machine code instructions.

People communicate instructions to the computer in symbolic languages and the easier this communication can be made the wider the application of computers will be. Scientists are already working on Artificial Intelligence and the next generation of computers may be able to understand human languages.

Instructions are written
in a high-level language
(e.g. Pascal, BASIC, COBOL, Ada, C, Lisp).
This is known as the source program.

▼

Compiler
Compilers translate the
original code into a
lower-level language or
machine code so that the
CPU can understand it.

▼

Instructions are compiled and packaged
into a program. The software is ready
to run on the computer.

4 Word building

A   **Look at the groups of words and decide what part of speech each word is. Then complete the sentences with the correct word.**

> compile   compiler   compilation

1   Programs written in a high-level language require .... , or translation into machine code.

2   A .... generates several low-level instructions for each source language statement.

3   Programmers usually .... their programs to create an object program and diagnose possible errors.

> program   programmers   programming   programmable

4   Most computer .... make a plan of the program before they write it. This plan is called a flowchart.

5   A computer .... is a set of instructions that tells the computer what to do.

6   Converting an algorithm into a sequence of instructions in a programming language is called ....

> bug   debug   debugger   debugging

7   New programs need .... to make them work properly.

8   Any error or malfunction of a computer program is known as a ....

9   The best compilers usually include an integrated .... which detects syntax errors.

B   **In the word *debug* the prefix *de-* is used. This prefix means 'to reverse an action'. Here are a few more examples:**

> defrost   debrief   declassify   decode   decompose   decentralize

Write down the base form of each verb. What do the verbs mean in your language? And what do the verbs with *de-* mean?

Can you think of any more verbs with *de-* in English?

5 Language work: Infinitive constructions

A Make sentences as in the example.

Example

not easy/write instructions in Pascal
It is not easy to write instructions in Pascal.

1 advisable/test the program under different conditions
2 expensive/set up a data-processing area
3 unusual for a program/work correctly the first time it is tested
4 difficult for students/learn FORTRAN
5 important/consider the capabilities of the programming language
6 quite easy/write instructions in BASIC

B Read the information in the HELP box and then look again at the reading passage in Task 3. Underline the infinitive constructions after modal verbs.

Example

Unfortunately, computers <u>cannot understand</u> ordinary spoken English …

C Look at these pairs of examples and decide where there is an 'important' change in meaning.

1 a I remember shutting down the computer before I left the room.
   b Please remember to buy the new program.
2 a They stopped to look at the flowchart.
   b They stopped looking at the flowchart.
3 a I like studying C language.
   b I like to study C language in the evenings.
4 a It has started to rain.
   b It has started raining.
5 a He needs to work harder.
   b This hard disk needs repairing.

HELP box
Infinitive constructions

The infinitive is used:

● after adjectives
  – It is **difficult to use** machine code.

● after modal verbs with *to: ought to, used to*
  – I **ought to make** a back-up copy.
  – Using a computer is much easier than it **used to be**.

● after modal and auxiliary verbs without *to:*
  can, could, may, might, shall, should, will, would, would rather, would sooner
  – Unfortunately, computers **can't understand** English.
  – I'**d rather buy** a game than a spreadsheet.

Unit 24 *Languages*

1 Warm-up

A Make a list of as many computer languages as you can think of.

B Study this table about Java and answer the questions below.

Language	Date	Characteristics	Uses
Java Invented by Sun Microsystems.	1995	Cross-platform language that can run on any machine. Small Java programs, called 'applets', let you watch animated characters, play music and interact with information.	Designed to create Internet applications. When you see a Web page containing Java links, a Java program is executed automatically.

1 Who invented Java?
2 When was Java developed?
3 Can Java run on any computer (Mac, PC or UNIX workstation)?
4 What are Java's small programs called? What can you do with them?

GAMELAN
Free Downloads
AnFX

Size: 535 KB
Date: 10/14/98
Platform: All
Requirements: 1 MB HD, IE 3 or 4 or Nav 2, 3 or 4
Licensing: Shareware
Author: Step Ahead Software

download now! **Buy It!**

AnFX lets anyone create impressive TV like commercials and information rich animations with moving fading objects using its point and click visual designer. AnFX animations are the most powerful yet quick to download Java based animations available. After the first page downloads, which takes less than a medium sized gif, subsequent pages work like lightning! Needs to be seen to be believed.

For more examples of Java, visit: www.gamelan.com

2 Language work: The passive

A Look at the HELP box and then complete these sentences with a suitable verb form.

1 COBOL (use) .... for business applications.
2 Original programs (write) .... in a high-level language.
3 All computer languages (must translate) .... into binary commands.
4 The ADA language (develop) .... in 1979.
5 In the 1970s, new languages such as LISP and PROLOG (design) .... for research into Artificial Intelligence.
6 A new version of TurboPascal (release) .... just ....
7 In the next century, computers (program) .... in natural languages like English or French.

> **HELP box**
> **The passive**
>
> The passive is formed with the verb *to be* in the correct tense and the past participle of the main verb.
>
> Instructions **are processed** by the CPU. The computer **was invented** by Charles Babbage.

B   How do you say the sentences in **A** in your language?

How do you make the passive in your language?

3 Speaking

Work in pairs. Student A: turn to page 145 and Student B: turn to page 149.

4 A short description of BASIC

Read the passage and complete it with verbs in brackets in the correct form.

BASIC is a general purpose high-level programming language, originally designed (1) (develop) .... programs in conversational mode. The name BASIC (2) (stand) .... for Beginner's All-purpose Symbolic Instruction Code. This language is (3) (find) .... on most microcomputers because it (4) (be) .... user-friendly and easy to learn.

BASIC (5) (consist) .... of two main parts: the **source language statements** – the instructions which form the program – and the **system commands** which (6) (allow) .... us to control and edit a program.

BASIC enables the user (7) (interact) .... with the program while it is being (8) (execute) ...., which means that data can be (9) (input) .... while the program is running. Each instruction is (10) (give) .... a line number which defines the logical sequence of statements within the program. Some well-known system commands in BASIC are: RUN, which executes a program (11) (hold) .... in a BASIC file; LIST, which prints a listing of a program on the screen; and DELETE, which (12) (remove) .... a program from a file.

A large number of PC manufacturers adopted BASIC. At present, however, there (13) (be) .... so many versions and extensions that programs written for one type of PC are not directly portable to another.

Microsoft **VISUALBASIC**

Programming System for Windows   STANDARD EDITION

Version 3.0! Now with built-in data access and OLE 2.0.

With built-in data access, OLE 2.0, and a FREE new guide to Visual Basic.

5 Listening

A 💿 **Listen to Vicky Cameron, the IT lecturer from Units 7 and 12, talking to her students about C language. Complete the table with the relevant information.**

Developed by	*Date*	*Characteristics*	*Uses*	*Extensions*
Dennis Ritchie at	....	Created to replace .... The language is small, ...	Originally designed for .... Today it is used to	C++ and .... Object-oriented languages.

B **Now write a paragraph describing C. You can start like this:**

C is a high-level programming language developed ...

```
#include <stdio.h>
main()
{
    printf("good morning\n");
}
```

This C program tells the computer to print the greeting 'good morning'

Unit 25 *The PostScript revolution*

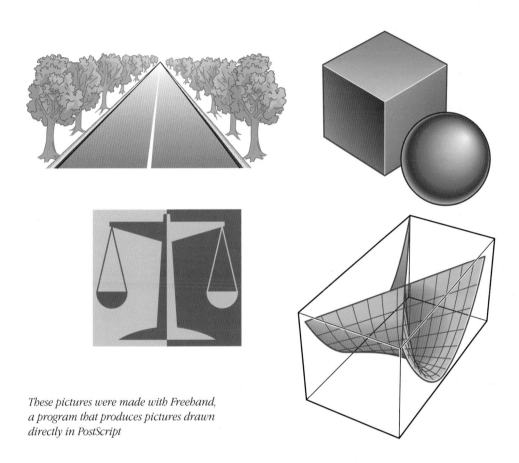

*These pictures were made with Freehand,
a program that produces pictures drawn
directly in PostScript*

1 Warm-up

A Look at the illustrations. What is PostScript? Choose the correct answer.

    a an application program
    b a page description language
    c hardware equipment

B Do you know any graphics programs that use PostScript commands?

**C Which of the following words are unfamiliar or unknown to you?
Underline them. Can you guess what they mean?**

device-independent	photosetter
output devices	resolution
PostScript interpreter	subroutine
drawing programs	EPS format

2 Reading

A **These statements are all false. Read the text and correct them.**

1 PostScript was created in the late 1980s.
2 The PostScript language is not understood by imagesetters.
3 The 'prolog' of a PostScript file contains the elements introduced by the user.
4 PostScript can only be used by Macintosh systems.
5 Laser printers don't need a PostScript interpreter to print pages in PostScript.
6 Non-PostScript programs give more precise control over drawing than PostScript programs.
7 PostScript pictures can't be exported.

What is PostScript?

In the past ten years the world of computers has witnessed the 'PostScript' revolution. PostScript was developed by Adobe Systems, Inc. in 1982 as a page description language for
5 printers like Apple LaserWriter and Allied Linotronic photosetters. Today it is used in most laser printers and is becoming a standard for high-quality type and graphics.

PostScript is mainly used to describe the
10 appearance of text, graphics and images on the printed page. It works in 'vectorial format', which means that it stores graphics not as images made up of dots but as geometric descriptions in equation form. This allows text
15 fonts and graphics to be enlarged or reduced with no loss of quality in the output.

A PostScript file consists of two main parts: the 'prolog' which contains a set of subroutines used to form different graphic elements (rectangles,
20 curves, etc.), and the 'script', which contains the elements introduced by the user. The script calls up the subroutines stored in the prolog and adds the parameters: for example, if you have drawn a square of 10 × 5 cm, the script calls up the
25 subroutine Square and specifies the values 10 × 5.

All the features of PostScript can be used with Macintosh, Windows or OS/2 environments. PostScript is device-independent, which means that it can speak to different output devices (printers, film recorders, imagesetters) and
30 adjust the quality of the final output to the highest capabilities of the output devices. You only need a PC able to send a file to an output device containing a PostScript interpreter. Each PostScript-based printer has a microprocessor, at
35 least 2 MB of RAM, and an operating system that interprets the PostScript code. In the case of imagesetters, the hardware that interprets the code is called a Raster Image Processor.

Some drawing programs can produce pictures
40 drawn in PostScript directly. These programs, such as Illustrator, Freehand or CorelDraw, can often give more precise control over drawing than non-PostScript packages. Pictures created in PostScript and saved as separate files (known
45 as Encapsulated PostScript (EPS) files) can be imported into a document generated by page-layout applications like Adobe PageMaker or QuarkXPress.

PostScript is an indispensable tool for illustrators,
50 graphic designers and DTP professionals. It has support for sound, video and other formats: you can rotate portions of the page, mix scanned images, specify halftone screens and introduce any number of effects. In fact, the only barrier is
55 your imagination.

B   Read the text again and deduce the meaning of the words you did not know in Task 1. Refer to the Glossary if you need to.

3 Vocabulary

'Script' in general English means 'something written' (although in some programming languages instructions are called 'scripts'). The word 'script' can be joined to other words to make new nouns. Look at the words below and decide which of them can be combined with 'script' to make a new noun.

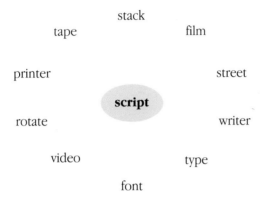

stack

tape   film

printer   street

script

rotate   writer

video   type

font

4 Language work: The past simple

A   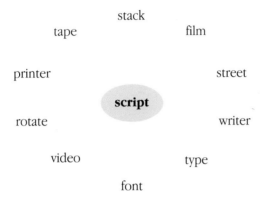 Look at the HELP box and then listen to these verbs. Put them in the right column.

developed	asked	described
decided	produced	supplied
watched	generated	published
persuaded	programmed	combined
scaled	interpreted	arranged

HELP box
The past simple

● Regular verbs add *-ed* to form the past simple (the affirmative form).

● Pronunciation of the '*-ed*'

The *-ed* is pronounced as:

– /t/ after voiceless sounds: /p/, /k/, /θ/, /s/, /f/, /ʃ/, /tʃ/: *stopped, talked*

– /d/ after voiced sounds: /b/, /g/, /ð/, /z/, /v/, /dʒ/, /l/, /r/, nasal consonants /m/, /n/, /ŋ/ and vowels: *visualized, plugged, specified*

– /ɪd/ after /t/ or /d/: *wanted, needed*

/t/	/d/	/ɪd/
....	....	....
....	....	....
....	....	....
....	....	....
....	....	....

B 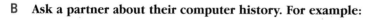 **Read the passage below and complete it with the verbs in the box. Then listen and check your answers.**

create	be	develop	test	publish	come out
have	offer	become	give	find	take

The PostScript language (1) .... in the early 1980s as a page description language for printers and photosetters. It was Adobe Systems, Inc. that (2) .... the PostScript language and developed Illustrator, the first program that (3) .... advantage of the full range of graphic possibilities (4) .... by PostScript. Adobe Systems (5) .... also the suppliers of fonts for use with PostScript-based printers.

The language was documented in *The PostScript Language Reference Manual*, (6) .... by Addison-Wesley in 1985. PostScript soon (7) .... widely used by DTP publishers and graphic designers. In 1990 PostScript level 2 (8) .... , which incorporated new features such as ATM technology, composite fonts, image compression and other details.

When some experts (9) .... the performance of different colour printers, they (10) .... that every PostScript printer .was easy to use and (11) .... consistently good results, while every non-PostScript printer (12) .... problems with output in at least one application.

5 Your experience with computers

A **Complete the chart below with notes about the different stages in your 'computer history'. For example: *1985: First used computer at school*. Add more boxes to the chart if you want to.**

Possible stages:

- first computer game
- first computer lesson at school/college
- first programming language learnt
- first software used
- first computer course/qualification
- first job involving computers
- first steps on the Internet

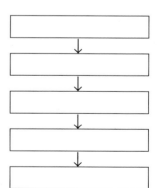

B **Ask a partner about their computer history. For example:**

'When did you first ...?'
'How long ago did you ...?'
'How old were you when you ...?'

C **Tell the rest of the class about your partner. Do most people in your group have similar computer histories?**

Unit 26 *Jobs in computing*

1 Reading

A Look carefully at the job advertisements and discuss with another student what personal qualities and professional abilities you would need for each job. Tick (✓) the most important qualities in the list. Then add some more of your own.

logical reasoning ☐   ability to lead a team ☐

imagination ☐   patience and tenacity ☐

physical fitness ☐   ability to draw well ☐

efficiency ☐   being good with figures ☐

self-discipline ☐   willingness to take on responsibility ☐

SENIOR PROGRAMMER
required by **DIGITUM**, a leading supplier of business systems to the insurance industry.

You will be able to work on the full range of development activities — analysis, design, coding, testing and implementation. At least two years' experience of COBOL is necessary.

As we are active in Europe, fluency in French, Italian or another European language is desirable.

Don't miss this opportunity to learn new skills and develop your career.

Send your curriculum vitae to
CHRIS SCOTT, PERSONNEL MANAGER,
DIGITUM, 75 PARKHILL STREET, LONDON SW2 3DE

You can visit our Web site at:
http://www.digitum.com

DTP Operator

required for a leading financial magazine. We are looking for a bright, competent QuarkXPress operator with at least three years' experience in design and layout. Skills in Photoshop, Freehand or Illustrator an advantage. Ability to work in a team and to tight deadlines is vital.

Please apply in writing, with CV and samples of your work, to Tom Parker, Production Manager, Financial Monthly, Stockton Street, London EC1 4WW

B Would you like to apply for one of these jobs? Why?

C **Study the personal profile of Charles Graham. Which is the most suitable job for him?**

Charles Graham
- 28 years old. Married.
- Education: 3 A-levels.
- In-depth knowledge of Apple Macintosh equipment.
- Course in graphic design and page-layout applications from Highland Art School.
- Proficient in Adobe PageMaker and SuperPaint.
- Diploma in word processing. Wide experience in MS Word and WordPerfect.
- Present job: Computer operator for PromoPrint, a company specializing in publishing catalogues and promotional material.

2 Language work: Past activities

A **Look at the HELP box and then complete the sentences below using *for*, *since* or *ago*.**

> **HELP box**
> ***for, since, ago***
>
> ***for:*** *We've used Microsoft Internet Explorer **for** two years.*
> ***since:*** *I've been a programmer **since** 1993.*
> ***ago:*** *I left university seven years **ago**.*

1 I've been looking for a job .... April.
2 They've used a fax machine .... the past two years.
3 Kate Jackson studied computer sciences .... three years.
4 I got married six years ....
5 She's been working for this firm .... 1990.

What is the difference in meaning between these two sentences?

a I've worked for a year as a senior programmer.
b I worked for a year as a senior programmer.

B Sarah Brown is one of the applicants for the job of Senior Programmer advertised in Task 1. Read her letter of application and put the verbs in brackets into the correct tense.

19 Sandford Street
London NW7 4HH

2 March 1999

Mr Scott
Personnel Manager
Digitum
75 Parkhill Street
London SW2 3DE

Dear Mr Scott,

I am writing to (1) (apply) .... for the position of Senior Programmer which (2) (advertise) .... on 28 February in *The Times*.

I (3) (work) .... as a computer programmer for the last three years. After graduation I (4) (work) .... for a year with NCR and (5) (be) .... now .... with Intelligent Software for two years. I design systems in COBOL for use in large retail chains. These have been very successful and we (6) (win) .... several new contracts in the UK and Europe on the strength of my team's success.

Last year I (7) (spend) .... three months in Spain testing our programs and also (8) (make) .... several short visits to Italy so I have a basic knowledge of Spanish and Italian. I now feel ready for more responsibility and more challenging work and would welcome the opportunity to learn about a new industry.

I enclose my curriculum vitae and look forward to hearing from you.

Yours sincerely,

Sarah Brown

Sarah Brown

3 Listening

A Listen to part of Chris Scott's interview with Sarah Brown and complete his notes.

Name: Sara Brown
Address: 19 Sandford Street, London NW7 4HH
Home phone no: 0181 569 1260
Job applied for: Senior Programmer
Qualifications:
– University: ....
– Foreign languages: Basic knowledge of Italian and Spanish

Work experience:
– At NCR ....
– What was software used for? ....
– What computers were used? ....
– Knowledge of databases? ....
– Present job: Works for Intelligent Software; writes programs in COBOL
Reasons for applying: ....

B Listen again and check your answers. Then compare your answers with a partner.

4 Writing

María Quintana, from Spain, is interested in the job of computer operator as advertised below. Use her notes to write a letter applying for the job.
You can start like this: *I'm writing to apply for …*

International Mercury
COMPUTERS

international
mercury
computers
37 Charles Place
London
SW10 6XX

requires Computer Operators

We have vacancies for experienced operators to work on their own initiative in a busy company. You will be responsible for the day-to-day running of our data-processing equipment.

You must be highly communicative and have good problem-solving skills. We can offer an excellent salary, training and good promotional prospects to the right candidate.

Send your CV and a covering letter to
James Taylor, International Mercury Computers,
37 Charles Place, London SW10 6XX
FAX 0171-323-0571

Notes for the Curriculum Vitae

— Cambridge Certificate of Proficiency in English
— Computer Sciences degree from Zaragoza University, Spain
— Knowledge of both Macintosh and Windows environments
— Two years' experience working on 'Linea Directa', a local magazine for computer users
— Present job: Computer operator for Graphic Color SL. This involves data control and editing, data preparation, and computer operating
— Reasons for applying: Want to develop operating skills and move into management

Computers tomorrow

7

Learning objectives

In this section you will learn how to:

- talk about different kinds of data communication systems: teletext, fax, local bulletin boards and the Internet
- describe the components and functions of a computer network, in oral and written form
- understand and discuss basic ideas about security and privacy on the Internet
- talk and write about new technologies
- understand how a pen computer works
- make predictions about the impact of computers on our lifestyle.

Unit 27 *Electronic communications*

1 Before you read

Try to answer these questions.

1 How can a PC be connected to another computer?
2 What data communication systems can you think of? Make a list.

2 Reading

A **Match the data communication services on the left with the requirements on
the right. Then read the passage and check your answers.**

1 fax	a To send a personal message to a
2 electronic mail (e-mail)	friend who is at a different workstation.
3 teletext	b To send a copy of a paper document –
4 local bulletin board system	for instance, a scientific article – from
(BBS)	Trento University to Cambridge University.
5 commercial online service	c To access massive databases containing
	all kinds of information, or to be connected
	with an airline reservations service.
	d To receive shareware and public domain
	programs from a user group.
	e To find out weather forecasts and sports
	information from the television.

Channels of communication

What are 'telecommunications'?

This term refers to the transmission of information over long distances using the telephone system, radio, TV, satellite or computer links. Examples are two people speaking on the phone, a sales department sending a fax to a client or someone reading the teletext pages on TV. But in the modern world, telecommunications mainly means transferring information from one PC to another via modem and phone lines (or fibre-optic cables).

What can you do with a modem?

A modem is your computer's link to the external world. With a modem you can exchange e-mail and files with friends and colleagues; you can access the Web and search for information about the stock market, current affairs, entertainment, etc.; you can participate in newsgroups and live conversations; you can make bank transactions and buy things from the comfort of your home. You can also access your office from your computer at home or your laptop in a hotel room.

Modems

Your PC is a digital device (it works with strings of 1s and 0s). However, the telephone system is an analogue device, designed to transmit the sounds and tones of the human voice. That's why we need a modem — a bridge between digital and analogue signals. The word 'modem' is an abbreviation of MOdulator/DEModulator. When a modem modulates, it sends very rapid on/off pulses. The computer on the other end translates (demodulates) those signals into intelligible text or graphics. Modem transmission speeds are measured in kilobits per second. Typical speeds are 28.8, 33.6 and 56 kbps

Today a lot of companies find it more efficient to have some employees doing their work at home. Using a modem, they transfer their work into the office where it is printed and distributed. The list of applications is endless.

What do you need to telecommunicate?

You just need a PC (or a terminal), a modem connected to the computer and the telephone line, and communication software. Once you have installed and configured your modem, you can communicate with people through bulletin boards and online services.

Local bulletin boards

Bulletin board systems (BBS) are frequently free because they are run by enthusiasts and sponsored by user groups or small businesses. The first time you make a BBS connection you are required to register your name, address, phone number and other information such as the kind of computer and modem you are using. The person who administers the BBS is called *sysop* (system operator). You can use a BBS to download artwork, games and programs, or you can participate in ongoing discussions. You can also upload (send) programs, but make sure they are shareware or public domain programs.

Online service providers

To gain access to the Internet you must first open an account with an Internet service provider (ISP) or a commercial online service provider. Both offer Internet access, but the latter provides exclusive services.

- **Internet service providers** usually offer access to the Web and newsgroups, an e-mail address, a program to download files from FTP sites, and IRC software so that you can have live chats with other users. Most ISPs charge a flat monthly or annual fee that gives you unlimited access to the Internet.

- The main **commercial online services** are America Online, CompuServe, Prodigy and

65 the Microsoft Network. They differ from dedicated ISPs in two ways: (1) they use a smooth, easy-to-use interface, and (2) they have extra services for members only (but they charge higher prices). For example, they offer airline reservations, professional forums, online shopping and stories for children. They also let you search their online encyclopaedias and special databases. 70

A *fax machine*
sends and receives copies of original documents via a phone line

Teletext *on ITV and Channel Four is an information service in Britain which broadcasts a database alongside the TV signal. It provides constantly updated and real time information*

B **Complete the sentences by using a term from the list. Then write the words in the crossword.**

| modem | network | online | download | newsgroups | services | account | telephone |

1 When you are connected to the Internet you are described as being ....

2 To communicate via the Internet you need a PC, a modem and a .... line.

3 To have access to the Internet you must first open an .... with an Internet service provider.

4 You need a .... to convert computer data into a form that can be transmitted over the phone lines.

5 The public discussion areas on the Internet are called ....

6 You can use a BBS to .... clip-art, games and shareware to your PC.

7 CompuServe and America Online offer exclusive .... to their customers.

8 The Internet is a global .... of computer networks.

C **Match and link the pairs of expressions that have the same meaning.**

file of structured data	BBS	facsimile machine	FTP	sysop
kilobits per second	system operator	modem	Internet relay chat
phone network	fax	database	bulletin board system	IRC
modulator/demodulator	file transfer protocol	kbps	telephone wires

3 Word building

A   **In pairs, look at the words below and decide:**

- what part of speech each word is
- where the stress falls on each item.

If you are not sure, look them up in a dictionary.

tele- means 'at/over a distance'

1 telegram	5 teletype	9 telegraphic	13 telescope
2 telephoto	6 teletext	10 telegraphically	14 telescopic
3 televise	7 telegraph	11 telepathy	15 telephonist
4 television	8 telegrapher	12 telepathic	

B   **Now write down some words formed by adding these prefixes.**

1   *auto-* (means 'self')
2   *trans-* (means 'across from one place to another')
3   *inter-* (means 'between', 'among')

4 Listening

A   **Look at the photo on page 128 and try to answer these questions.**

1   What is a cybercafé?
2   What services would you expect when entering a cybercafé?

B   ▣◉ **Listen to this interview with Daniel Sturdy, the manager of an Internet café in London. Then say whether these sentences are true (T) or false (F).**

1   A cybercafé is a café where you can have access to the Internet and related services. ☐
2   You can talk to people over the Internet as if you were speaking on the phone. ☐
3   They don't help people who have problems while using the Internet. ☐
4   A private e-mail account costs £10 a month. ☐
5   At the moment they have got many international users. ☐
6   You have to pay long-distance rates on the Internet. ☐
7   In the café area you can sit, drink coffee and chat to people. ☐
8   Most of the computers are in an upstairs area. ☐

A London cybercafé

C Mini-project: Plan your own cybercafé!

Imagine you want to open an Internet café in town. In pairs, look at the HELP box and make a project about a café.

HELP box

Consider the following:

- the **money** you need to set up and run your cybercafé
- the kind of **visitors** you would like to have
- the **location** (try to find a place accessible to people who are likely to use a cybercafé)
- the **services** you want to offer (food, drinks, coffees, etc.)
- the type of **furniture**
- the things that can help you create a **relaxing atmosphere** (music, decoration, lighting, private areas, chess and card games, etc.)
- whether you want to have second-hand **books**, classic literature or **magazines** about computers and the Internet.

Make decisions about:

- the type of Internet connection: via a modem (carrying data at 56 kbps), an ISDN line (at 128 kbps), a T-1 line (at 1,544 kbps) or a high-speed T-3 connection (at 44,736 kbps)
- hardware equipment (Macs and PCs, printer, fax, etc.)
- software (web browser, e-mail, online chatting, games on CD-ROMs, etc.)
- how much you will charge customers for your services
- introductory and advanced classes for users.

Now choose a name and a slogan for your cybercafé.

Unit 28 *Internet issues*

1 Warm-up

A **Try to answer these questions.**

1 Is it technically possible for computer criminals to infiltrate into the Internet and steal sensitive information?
2 What is a hacker?
3 Can viruses enter your PC from the Internet?

B **Match these texts with the correct pictures.**

1 Web browsers warn you if the connection is not secure; they display a message when you try to send personal information to a server.
2 Private networks use a software and hardware mechanism, called a 'firewall', to block unauthorized traffic from the Internet.

3 You have to type your user name and password to access a locked computer system or network.
4 An open padlock in Netscape Communicator indicates the page is not secure; a closed padlock indicates the page is encrypted (secure).

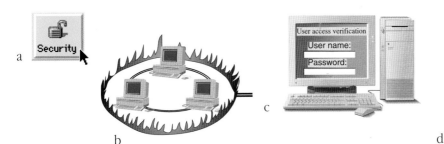

a b c

d

2 Reading

A **Read the text on page 130 and find answers to these questions.**

1 Why is security so important on the Internet?
2 What security features are offered by Netscape Communicator and Internet Explorer?
3 What security standard is used by most banks to make online transactions secure?
4 How can we protect and keep our e-mail private?
5 What methods are used by companies to make internal networks secure?
6 Which ways can a virus enter a computer system?

Security and privacy on the Internet

There are a lot of benefits from an open system like the Internet, but we are also exposed to hackers who break into computer systems just for fun, as well as to steal information or propagate viruses. So how do you go about making online transactions secure?

Security on the Web

The question of security is crucial when sending confidential information such as credit card numbers. For example, consider the process of buying a book on the Web. You have to type your credit card number into an order form which passes from computer to computer on its way to the online bookstore. If one of the intermediary computers is infiltrated by hackers, your data can be copied. It is difficult to say how often this happens, but it's technically possible.

To avoid risks, you should set all security alerts to high on your Web browser. Netscape Communicator and Internet Explorer display a lock when the Web page is secure and allow you to disable or delete 'cookies'.

If you use online bank services, make sure your bank uses digital certificates. A popular security standard is SET (secure electronic transactions).

E-mail privacy

Similarly, as your e-mail message travels across the net, it is copied temporarily on many computers in between. This means it can be read by unscrupulous people who illegally enter computer systems.

The only way to protect a message is to put it in a sort of 'envelope', that is, to encode it with some form of encryption. A system designed to send e-mail privately is *Pretty Good Privacy*, a freeware program written by Phil Zimmerman.

Network security

Private networks connected to the Internet can be attacked by intruders who attempt to take valuable information such as Social Security numbers, bank accounts or research and business reports.

To protect crucial data, companies hire security consultants who analyse the risks and provide security solutions. The most common methods of protection are passwords for access control, encryption and decryption systems, and firewalls.

Virus protection

Viruses can enter a PC through files from disks, the Internet or bulletin board systems. If you want to protect your system, don't open e-mail attachments from strangers and take care when downloading files from the Web. (Plain text e-mail alone can't pass a virus.)

Remember also to update your anti-virus software as often as possible, since new viruses are being created all the time.

HELP box

- **hacker:** a person who obtains unauthorized access to computer data
- **cookies:** small files used by Web servers to know if you have visited their site before
- **certificates:** files that identify users and Web servers on the net, like digital identification cards
- **encryption:** the process of encoding data so that unauthorized users can't read it
- **decryption:** the process of decoding encrypted data transmitted to you

B **Complete these sentences by using a term from the text. Then write the words in the puzzle.**

1 Users have to enter a p......................... to gain access to a network.

2 You can download a lot of f......................... or public domain programs from the net.

3 Hundreds of h......................... break into computer systems every year.

4 A computer v......................... can infect your files and corrupt your hard disk.

5 The process of encoding data so that unauthorized users can't read the data is known as e......................... .

6 A f......................... is a device which allows limited access to an internal network from the Internet.

7 You can include an a......................... as part of your e-mail message.

8 This company uses d......................... techniques to decode (or decipher) secret data.

3 Listening

Listen to Diana Wilson, a member of the Internet Safety Foundation. She is talking about cyberspace's dangers and benefits for children. Complete the notes in this table.

Benefits

● The Internet brings benefits for
  (1)......................... and entertainment.

Risks

● manipulation of children
● invasions of (2).........................
● child (3) ....
● violence and neo-Nazi (4) ....

Solutions

● There are Web sites (5) ....
  for children.
● Internet (6) .... programs let
  parents block objectionable Web sites.
● Web sites should (7) .... their
  content with a label, from child-friendly
  to over 18-only.

But this may limit free expression.

Cyber Patrol, a popular Internet filter.
http://www.cyberpatrol.com

4 Hackers!

Read the text in order to answer these questions.

1 Which hacking case inspired the film *War Games*?
2 Why was Nicholas Whitely arrested in 1988?
3 How old was the hacker that cracked the US defence computer in October 1989?
4 Who was known as 'Dark Dante' on the networks? What was he accused of?
5 Which computer club showed on TV a way to attack bank accounts?

Sept '70	John Draper, also known as Captain Crunch, discovers that the penny whistle offered in boxes of Cap'n Crunch breakfast cereal perfectly generates the 2,600 cycles per second (Hz) signal that AT&T used to control its phone network at the time. He starts to make free calls.
Aug '74	Kevin Mitnick, a legend among hackers, begins his career, hacking into banking networks and destroying data, altering credit reports of his enemies, and disconnecting the phone lines of celebrities. His most famous exploit – hacking into the North American Defense Command in Colorado Springs – inspired *War Games*, the 1983 movie.
Jul '81	Ian Murphy, a 23-year-old known as Captain Zap on the networks, gains instant notoriety when he hacks into the White House and the Pentagon.
Dec '87	IBM international network is paralysed by hacker's Christmas message.
Jul '88	Union Bank of Switzerland 'almost' loses £32 million to hacker-criminals. Nicholas Whitely is arrested in connection with virus propagation.
Oct '89	Fifteen-year-old hacker cracks US defence computer.
Nov '90	Hong Kong introduces anti-hacking legislation.
Aug '91	Israelis arrest 18-year-old for hacking foreign banking and credit card networks.
Jul '92	In New York, five teenagers are charged with breaking into computer sytems at several regional phone companies, large firms and universities.
Dec '92	Kevin Poulsen, known as 'Dark Dante' on the networks, is charged with stealing tasking orders relating to an Air Force military exercise. He is accused of theft of US national secrets and faces up to 10 years in jail.
Feb '97	German Chaos Computer Club shows on TV the way to electronically obtain money from bank accounts using a special program on the Web.
May '98	Computer criminals propagate a lot of viruses through the Internet.

5 Language work: The past simple (revision)

Look at the text in Task 4 again and put the verbs into the past.

Example

*In September 1970, John Draper discover**ed** that the penny whistle … generat**ed** … He start**ed** to make free calls.*

Unit 29   *LANs and WANs*

1 Warm-up

Try to answer these questions.

1 What is a computer network?
2 What are the benefits of connecting computers and peripherals in a network?

2 Listening

Listen to the description of this computer network. Label the different elements.

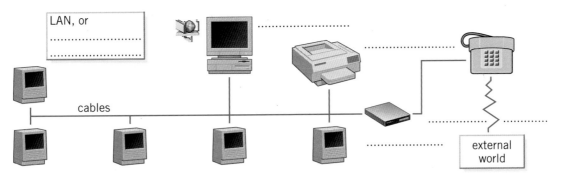

3 Reading

Read the text on page 134, then match the technical terms on the left with the explanations on the right.

1 LAN	a the hardware that emits and receives signals in a computer network
2 network architecture	b a network contained in a relatively small area
3 nodes	c the arrangement of nodes in a communication system (i.e. the distribution of elements in a network)
4 protocol	d a device that translates protocols between different types of networks (e.g. it can link networks of PCs and Macs to mainframes and minicomputers)
5 transceiver	
6 token	
7 gateway	e a special unit of data which acts as a key on a Token Ring network; only the machine in possession of this piece of software can transmit on the network
	f a set of rules that allows the exchange of information over a network
	g computer devices interconnected in a network

Network configurations

A **network** is a group of devices (PCs, printers, etc.) or 'nodes' connected by communications circuits so that users can share data, programs and hardware resources. A network has two main elements: the **physical structure** that links the equipment and the **software** that allows communication.

The physical distribution of nodes and their circuits is known as network 'topology' or 'architecture'. The software consists of the **protocols**, i.e. the rules which determine the formats by which information may be exchanged between different systems. We could say that cables and transceivers (the architecture) allow computers to 'hear' one another, while the software is the 'language' that they use to 'talk' to one another over the network.

As regards the cables, they consist essentially of the transceiver – the hardware that sends and receives network signals. At present the most widely used transceivers are Token Ring, Ethernet and LocalTalk. Token Ring is the most common method of connecting PCs and IBM mainframes. Most Token Ring adapters transmit data at a speed of 16 megabits per second. With Ethernet, data is transmitted at 100 Mbits/sec. Ethernet provides a very robust, trouble-free architecture with good levels of performance. *In this regard,* Ethernet is the best solution for fast and intensive activity.

LocalTalk transceivers are the cheapest of all because they are directly included in each Macintosh. However, they're a bit slow, which is why most Macs come with built-in Ethernet.

As for protocols, these are rules which describe things like transmission speed and physical interfaces. The Token Ring protocol avoids the possibility of collisions. To transmit data, a workstation needs a **token**, and as there is only one token per network, holding one guarantees sole use of the network. With Ethernet there are other options, of which TCP/IP (Transmission Control Protocol/Internet Protocol) is perhaps the most useful since it allows different operating systems to communicate with each other. *With regard to* LocalTalk networks, they use AppleTalk protocols. The Macintosh operating system includes the AppleTalk manager and a set of drivers that let programs on different Macs exchange information.

LANs can be interconnected by gateways. These devices help manage communications and control traffic on large networks. They change the data to make it compatible with the protocols of different networks.

4 Language work: Prepositional phrases of 'reference'

In the sentence *As for protocols, these are rules ...,* the expression *as for* marks the theme of the sentence.

Look at the words in the box below and combine them to make nine similar phrases of reference meaning 'concerning'. You can use words more than once. Look back at the text to find some of them.

with	to	in	for	as	on	the	regard
this	regards	matter	reference	of	respect		

5 Writing

A   The diagram below illustrates the computer connections in three areas of a large company. Read the description of the office area network. Then write similar descriptions of the other two areas.

In the **office area,** the computers are connected in a Token Ring network. Various PCs have access to a file server, an IBM mainframe, an e-mail server and a printer.
The file server probably contains application programs like databases, spreadsheets and accounting packages. The mainframe contains large amounts of information about the company, administration work, etc.

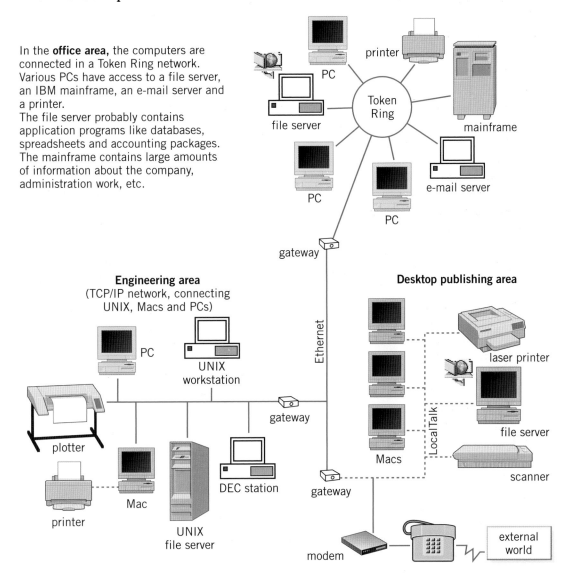

B   If you use a network write a short description of it, with details of its architecture and protocol. Say what you and your colleagues use the network for.

6 WANs and worldwide communications

Try to answer these questions.

1 What is a WAN?
2 How can computers be linked up over a long distance?
3 What are the advantages of optical-fibre cables over telephone lines?
4 What is the function of communications satellites?

Now read the passage and find out if your answers were correct.

For long-distance or worldwide communications, computers and LANs are usually connected into a wide area network (WAN) to form a single, integrated network. Two good examples of wide area networks are Internet and Arpanet. They transfer data and e-mail for university researchers and academics, commercial groups, military installations and ordinary people.

Networks can be linked together by either **telephone lines** or **fibre-optic cables**. For example, ISDN (integrated services digital network) is an international standard for transmitting digital text, sound, voice and video data over telephone lines. On the other hand, FDDI (fibre distributed data interface) is an optical-fibre network. This new standard transmits data at great speed – 100 megabits per second.

Modern telecommunications use fibre-optic cables because data can be transmitted at a very high speed through the extremely wide bandwidths of glass fibres. The fibre system operates by transmitting light pulses at high frequencies along the glass fibre. This offers considerable advantages: (i) the cables require little physical space; (ii) they are safe because they don't carry electricity; (iii) they avoid electromagnetic interference.

Networks on different continents can also be connected via **satellite**. Computers are connected by a modem either to ordinary telephone wires or fibre-optic cables, which are linked to a dish aerial. This aerial has a large concave reflector for the reception and sending of signals. Then, when signals are received by the satellite, they are amplified and sent on to workstations in another part of the world.

Libraries use a WAN to keep records of loans and to supply information to library users who have modems

7 Speaking

**In small groups, study and discuss the illustration below. Then prepare a
description and give an oral report to the class.**

● This diagram represents a wide area network or WAN. Two networks are linked via
satellite. One network is in .... and consists of ....
.... The other LAN is in .... and
contains ....

● In Los Angeles, the computers are connected to the telephone lines by ....
However, in Barcelona ....

● The satellite receives signals from .... Then the signals are
retransmitted to ....

● The purpose of this integrated network may be ....
.... It allows large
companies and institutions to ....
....

Unit 30 *New technologies*

1 New products

A **Look at these pictures and match them with texts 1 to 4.**

a ....

b ....

c ....

d ....

WORLDGATE

tv listings

e-mail

web

setup

TV

my town

weather

news

sports

1 Smart phones for sending and receiving voice, e-mail, and Internet data are already available. One example is *Mobile*Access, the wireless phone from Mitsubishi. The software from Unwired Planet connects you to a server, displaying a directory of databases and information services.

   You can connect *Mobile*Access to your laptop and use its modem to access the Internet. The technology is based on the cellular digital packet data (CDPD) protocol.

2 Internet TV sets allow you to surf the Web and have e-mail while you are watching TV, or vice versa. Imagine watching a film on TV and simultaneously accessing a Web site where you get information on the actors in the film. This is ideal for people who are reluctant to use PCs but are interested in the Internet.

   WebTV was the first company which brought Internet services to TV viewers through a set-top computer box. Another option is WorldGate's technology, which offers the Internet through cable TV.

   The model built by OEM Metec integrates a complete Windows PC in a TV set. The next generation of Internet-enabled televisions will incorporate a smart-card for home shopping, banking and other interactive services.

3 Virtual reality lets people interact with artificial objects and environments through three-dimensional computer simulation. In a VR system, you are hooked to a computer through a controlling device, such as a glove, and head-mounted displays give you the feeling of being propelled into an artificial three-dimensional world. The computer brings to life events in a distant, virtual world using databases or real-time objects and sounds. Your senses are immersed in an illusionary, yet sensate, world.

   VR can be applied to anything from video games, testing a motor vehicle, visiting a virtual exhibition, to checking out imaginary kitchen designs.

4 Video teleconferencing is a new technology that allows organizations to create 'virtual' meetings with participants in multiple locations.

   A video teleconferencing system combines data, voice and video. Participants see colour images of each other, accompanied by audio, and they can exchange textual and graphical information.

   In video teleconferencing, images are captured by computer-mounted cameras. Video processors digitize and compress the images, which are transmitted over a network bidirectionally. Data and sound travel via telephone lines.

B **Write a suitable caption under each picture.**

C **Match the terms on the left with the explanations on the right.**

1 Internet-enabled TV
2 Web site
3 virtual reality
4 to compress files
5 video teleconferencing
6 wireless smart phone

a location on the Internet where a company puts Web pages

b technology that integrates data, sound and video: participants in different/distant virtual places hold a meeting as if they were face to face

c to squeeze data into smaller files by coding it into specific formats that take less space

d TV set used as an Internet device

e technology that allows users to see a computer-simulated world in which they can move

f device that can send and receive voice or data without the use of wire

2 Get ready for listening

**Look at the computer in the photo and answer
the questions about it.**

1 What is different about this computer?
2 How do you enter information?
3 What kind of screen do you think it has: a cathode
   ray tube (CRT) or a liquid-crystal display (LCD)?
4 What sort of power supply do you think it uses?
5 If you had one, what would you do with it?

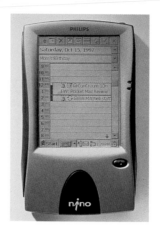

3 Listening

A ☰◉ **Listen to this interview with Tom Bryant, a writer with a computer
magazine. Are the following sentences true (T) or false (F)?**

1 A pen-based interface uses an electronic stylus as an input device. ☐

2 Pen computers do not require specialized operating systems
   to recognize pen gestures and characters. ☐

3 Pen computers come with operating systems that can be trained
   to recognize handwriting. ☐

4 Some pen computers are more powerful than desktop PCs. ☐

5 A personal digital assistant is a hand-held pen computer designed
   to organize and communicate personal information. ☐

6 You cannot transmit data from pen computers to desktop PCs
   and peripherals. ☐

7 Business people will make up a large section of the pen
   computer market. ☐

B **Read this extract from the interview and fill in the missing words.
The first letter of each missing word is given.**

Interviewer: Can you explain how a (1) p.................................... computer works?

Tom Bryant: Sure. A pen computer usually (2) r.................................. on
               rechargeable batteries. You hold the computer with one hand and
               with the other you use an electronic (3) s........................ to write, draw
               and make selections on a flat LCD (4) s........................ .

Interviewer: That means it doesn't have a keyboard.

Tom Bryant: That's right. You write (5) i.................................... with the stylus like
               a pen.

Interviewer: And how does the computer (6) r.................................... what
               you write?

Tom Bryant: It reads the (7) p.................................... of the pen and sends signals to
               the screen. The computer then translates the movements of the pen

into characters or performs the functions like 'delete'. The operating system recognizes specific gestures like drawing a circle or crossing out a (8) w.................................. .

Interviewer: Can these operating systems really recognize
(9) h.................................. ?

Tom Bryant: Yes, they can be trained to recognize (10) c....................................
written in your own handwriting. A lot of hand-held computers use
Microsoft Windows CE or the Palm OS from Palm Computing.

Now listen again and check your answers.

C   **How do you say these expressions in your language?**

1   rechargeable batteries
2   a flat LCD screen
3   a pen-based interface
4   handwriting recognition

5   a Personal Digital Assistant
6   an infra-red port
7   a portable supplement

4 Discussion

Look at the picture below and read the text. Then discuss these questions in small groups, and prepare a short report for the class.

1   What are the most important differences between hand-held computers (e.g. palmtops, PDAs, etc.) and traditional computers?
2   What are the advantages and limitations of hand-held computers?
3   Should students be allowed to use hand-held computers in class?
4   Do you agree with this statement: 'Soon, hand-held PCs will combine the functions of traditional PCs, cellular phones and pocket-size organizers'?

Psion Series 5 hand-held computers have a keyboard and a touch-sensitive screen. Although very light weight, they have a 35 hour battery capacity, 8 MB of RAM, a windowing OS, a microphone for sound recording, and a full range of applications. PsiMail Internet software lets you send e-mail and browse the Web. It has a fast serial port interface to computers, modems and printers

5 Language work: Making predictions

A **Look at the HELP box and then expand these sentences using the future perfect tense.**

1 In ten years' time/a lot of people/connect their television to the telephone line
2 Portable computers/replace/ desktop computers/in a few years' time
3 With the help of computers/ doctors/find/cure/AIDS and cancer/by the year 2005
4 By this time next year/software manufacturers/make/hundreds of new programs
5 By 2020/post offices and bookshops/disappear
6 By this time next year/I/buy/ pen computer

HELP box
Making predictions

- Future with *will/shall*
  A computer program will be the world chess champion.

- Future continuous (*will be* + present participle)
  In twenty years' time, some people will be living in space, inside a computerized colony.

- Future perfect (*will have* + past participle)
  By 2020, new technology will have revolutionized communications.

- Special structures
  – Possibility (*may/might/could*)
    Scientists may discover new electronic components.
  – Probability (*likely to*)
    Talking machines are likely to be built.
  – Certainty (*certainly, definitely, certain to*)
    Working hours will definitely become shorter with the help of computers. Prices are certain to go up.

B **Here are some predictions made by an intelligent supercomputer. In small groups, write your own predictions.**

- Work/Jobs
  e.g. *By the year 2030 human labour in industry will have been replaced by robots.*
  Yours: ....
  ....

- Homes
  e.g. *Families will have robots to do the housework.*
  Yours: ....
  ....

- Education/Schools
  e.g. *By the end of the next century, every student in every school in the world will have a PC.*
  Yours: ....
  ....

- Money/Holidays
  e.g. *Most families will have videotex systems, with which they can shop and make financial transactions. Cash will disappear.*
  Yours: ....
  ....

I GUESS I JUST CAN'T FACE THE FUTURE....

PSYCHIATRY

BLOWER

Notes for Student A

Unit 6 Task 4 Speaking

**Read these notes about two input devices. Then describe them to your partner.
They have to guess what you are describing.**

1 ● scans text and pictures
   ● sends digitized image to computer

2 ● allows you to control computer vocally
   ● spoken commands do what is normally done with keyboard/mouse

Now listen to your partner and guess which input device they are describing.

Unit 20 Task 6 Speaking

**Look at the graph below and describe it to your partner. Then answer your
partner's questions.**

Useful constructions

This is a two-/three-dimensional representation of ...
In 1998, they paid £ ... for ...
They spent £ ... on ...
As for ..., that cost them ...

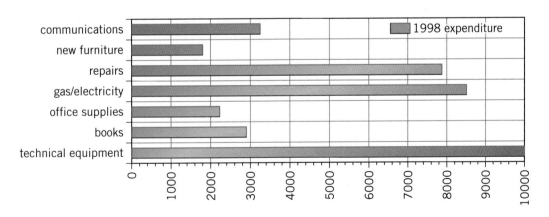

Graph 1   The 1998 expenditure of Lancashire College expressed in pounds

Now look at this graph and listen to your partner's description of it.
Ask questions so that you can complete the graph.

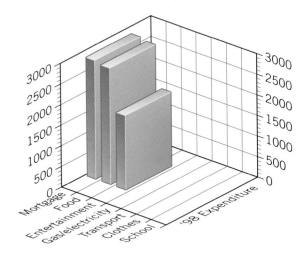

Graph 2   The 1998 expenditure of the Brown family expressed in pounds

Unit 21 Task 5   Computers for newspapers

Read the information on the next page which Katherine Powell received from *El Independiente* and tell your partner about:

● the hardware used to produce the newspaper:
  – computers on the network
  – printers
  – data communication systems

● the software used to:
  – edit text
  – create illustrations
  – manipulate photographs
  – design the pages.

El Independiente

- Hardware:
- The newspaper is written and edited on PCs and Macintosh computers.
- Several MicroVAX servers (with 128 MB of RAM and 6 GB hard disk) are dedicated to managing communications on the network and storing common files.
- Black-and-white proofs are printed by Epson ink-jet and laser printers. The final product is printed by photosetters (imagesetters).
- Different data communications systems — fax machines, e-mail, etc. — are used to communicate with newspaper correspondents. There is a Web edition published on the Internet.

- Software
- The text is typed and edited with compatible word processors.
- The illustrations (diagrams, charts, etc.) are created with Freehand and Illustrator.
- The photographs are corrected with Adobe Photoshop (image manipulation software).
- The page-layout is designed with QuarkXPress. The text is imported and flowed into columns. The artwork and graphics are imported, resized, cropped and placed in the layout.
- The files are converted into HTML code and displayed on the Web.

Your partner has the information which another newspaper – *Le Matin* – sent to Katherine Powell. Listen to your partner tell you about it and complete the fact file below.

Le Matin

- The hardware used to produce the newspaper:
  - computers on the network: ....
  ....
  - peripherals: ....
  - data communication systems: ....
- The software used to:
  - edit text: ....
  - produce graphics: ....
  - arrange text and pictures on the page: ....
  - design Web pages: ....

Unit 24 Task 3   Speaking

Complete the table on the next page by asking for information, like this:

- What does 'COBOL' mean?
- 'COBOL' stands for ...
- When was it developed?

- In …
- What's it used for?
- It's used for …
- What features has it got?
- It is easy to use and it's written in English. It can handle very large data files.

Answer your partner's questions too.

Computer language	Date	Characteristics	Uses
COBOL (**CO**mmon **B**usiness **O**riented **L**anguage)	1958–59	Easy to read. Able to handle very large files. Written in English.	Mainly used for business applications.
BASIC	....	....	General purpose language. Used to teach programming.
Pascal (named after ....)	1970–73	Structured language with algorithmic features designed for fast execution of the object program. A fast compiler called TurboPascal was created in 1982 — very popular.	....
LOGO	1969	....	Designed for use in schools to encourage children to experiment with programming.
HTML (................................ ....)	1990	HTML codes control the use of fonts and images on a Web page and specify the links to other Internet sites. HTML files are viewed with a client program called a 'browser'.	....

Notes for Student B

Unit 6 Task 4   Speaking

Listen to your partner and guess which input devices they are describing.

Now use these notes to describe two input devices to Student A.

1 ● stationary device
   ● controls the cursor and selects items on the screen
   ● works like upside-down mouse
   ● ball on top turned round with fingers

2 ● graphics tool
   ● lets you interact with computer
   ● you move pressure-stylus across the surface of a tablet
   ● creates graphics

Unit 20 Task 6   Speaking

**Look at this graph and listen to your partner's description of it.
Ask questions so that you can complete the graph.**

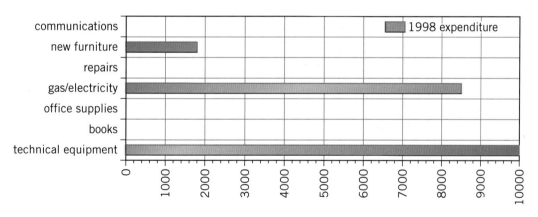

Graph 1   The 1998 expenditure of Lancashire College expressed in pounds

Now look at this graph and describe it to your partner. Then answer your partner's questions.

Useful constructions

This is a two-/three-dimensional representation of ...
In 1998, they paid £ ... for ...
They spent £ ... on ...
As for ..., that cost them ...

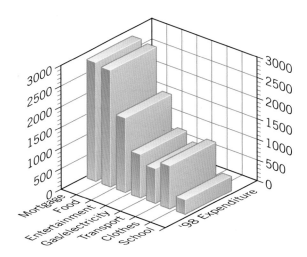

Graph 2   The 1998 expenditure of the Brown family expressed in pounds

Unit 21 Task 5   Computers for newspapers

Your partner has the information which *El Independiente* sent to Katherine Powell. Listen to your partner tell you about it and complete the fact file below:

El Independiente

● the hardware used to produce the newspaper:
  – computers on the network: ....
  ....
  – printers: ....
  – data communication systems: ....
● the software used to:
  – edit text: ....
  – create illustrations: ....
  – manipulate photographs: ....
  – design the pages: ....

Katherine Powell also sent a similar letter to *Le Matin*.
Read the information they provided and tell your partner about:

- the hardware used to produce the newspaper:
  - computers on the network
  - peripherals
  - data communication systems

- the software used to:
  - edit text
  - produce graphics
  - arrange text and pictures on the page
  - design Web pages.

- **Hardware:**
  - The system is based on the Ethernet network: several PCs are connected to a file server Pentium III running at 500 MHz with a capacity of 16 GB.
  - All kinds of peripherals are interconnected over the network (scanners, laser printers, photosetters, faxes, etc.).
  - The newspaper is connected via a modem to other papers of the 'Z' group.
  - Photographs are received via satellite.
  - There is a Web edition on our Internet site.

- **Software:**
  - The text is written and edited with WordPerfect word-processing software.
  - The graphics are produced on Macintosh computers with commercial packages such as Adobe Illustrator and Canvas from Deneba Systems.
  - Words, pictures, graphs and tables are imported and arranged on the page by Ventura Publisher, a DTP package.
  - The Web pages are designed with FrontPage, an HTML editor.

Unit 24 Task 3   Speaking

Complete the table on the next page by asking for information, like this:

- What does 'COBOL' mean?
- 'COBOL' stands for …
- When was it developed?
- In …
- What's it used for?
- It's used for …
- What features has it got?
- It is easy to use and it's written in English. It can handle very large data files.

Answer your partner's questions too.

Computer language	Date	Characteristics	Uses
COBOL (**CO**mmon **B**usiness **O**riented **L**anguage)	1958–59	Easy to read. Able to handle very large files. Written in English.	Mainly used for business applications.
.... (**B**eginner's **A**ll-purpose **S**ymbolic **I**nstruction **C**ode)	1964–65	High-level programming language. Interactive. Easy to learn. Displays error messages that help users to correct mistakes. Has a large number of dialects.	....
Pascal (named after the famous scientist Blaise Pascal)	1970–73	....	General purpose. Often used in colleges and universities to teach programming.
LOGO	....	Easy to learn. Flexible — it can do maths, make lists, construct graphs, etc. Its drawing capabilities allow children to construct simple graphics programs.	....
.... (**H**yper**T**ext **M**arkup **L**anguage)	....	....	Used to create hypertext documents that can be displayed on the Web.

Glossary

A

acceleration card /ək‚selə'reɪʃən ‚kɑːd/ *n* A board that increases the speed of the processor.

access time /'ækses ‚taɪm/ *n* The average time required for the read/write head to move and have access to data; measured in milliseconds. Also known as 'seek time'.

acoustic coupler /ə‚kuːstɪk 'kʌplə(r)/ *n* A type of modem which allows an ordinary telephone receiver to be used for connecting a computer to the telephone network.

ADA /'eɪdə/ A programming language developed for the US Department of Defense, named after Lord Byron's daughter Augusta Ada, who worked with Charles Babbage and is not unjustly described as the first programmer.

additive colour /'ædɪtɪv ‚kʌlə/ *n* A colour model on cathode ray tube displays.

address /ə'dres/ *n* A code number that identifies the location of stored information.

Adobe Systems /ə'dəʊbɪ ‚sɪstəmz/ Creators of the PostScript language and the Illustrator application, and suppliers of fonts for use with PostScript printers.

algorithm /'ælgərɪðm/ *n* A series of instructions or a step-by-step procedure for the solution of a problem.

alias /'eɪlɪæs/ *n* A nickname that refers to a person or a list of persons on the net.

animation /‚ænɪ'meɪʃən/ *n* The process of creating and recording images that change over time.

applets /'æpləts/ *n* Small applications written in Java. When you display a Web page with Java links, a Java applet is executed automatically.

application generator /‚æplɪ'keɪʃən ‚dʒenəreɪtə/ *n* A tool that allows applications to be created interactively. Frequently includes a fourth-generation language and a database management system.

application program /‚æplɪ'keɪʃən ‚prəʊɡræm/ *n* A program which executes a specific task, such as word processing, database management or financial planning.

ARPANet /'ɑːpənet/ *n* Advanced Research Projects Agency Network, developed in the early 70s by the US Department of Defense. This network is the precursor to the Internet.

arithmetic logic unit (ALU) /ə‚rɪθmətɪk 'lɒdʒɪk juːnɪt/ *n* A component of the CPU which performs the actual arithmetic and logical operations asked for by a program.

arrow keys /'ærəʊ ‚kiːz/ *n* Direction or cursor keys that allow the user to move the insertion point around the screen.

assembler /ə'semblə(r)/ *n* A special program that converts a program written in a low-level language into machine code.

assembly language /ə'semblɪ 'læŋwɪdʒ/ *n* A low-level language in which instructions are the mnemonic equivalent of the code understood by the machine. Used for specialized applications where speed or compactness of code is the most important consideration.

AT-compatible /‚eɪˌtiː kəm'pætəbəl/ *adj* A computer which can run the same software as the IBM PC-AT, the model introduced by IBM in 1984.

attachment /ə'tætʃmənt/ *n* A file that has been included as part of an e-mail message.

attributes /'ætrɪbjuːts/ *n* Characteristics that affect the visual representation of lines and polygons, e.g. line styles, rectangle colour, etc.

authentication /ɔː‚θentɪ'keɪʃən/ *n* A security measure used to verify the user's identity on the net. When you configure the PPP program to access the Internet you have to enter a password and the user identification number.

avatar /‚ævə'tɑː/ *n* An object which represents a participant in a three-dimensional chat room.

B

backbone /'bækbəʊn/ *n* High-speed lines or connections that form the major access pathways within the Internet.

backing store /'bækɪŋ ‚stɔː/ *n* A storage device with a larger capacity but slower access time than the main memory. This type of memory is stable. It can be in the form of hard disks, floppy disks, tapes or optical disks.

back-up /'bækʌp/ *n* A copy of data or software, usually kept in case the original disk is damaged.

back up /bæk 'ʌp/ *v* To copy files from one disk to another.

bandwidth /'bændwɪdθ/ *n* The quantity of data that can be transmitted through a network. It is measured in bits per second (bps).

batch processing /'bætʃ ‚prəʊsesɪŋ/ *n* A method of information processing in which transactions are prepared for input to the computer for processing as a single unit. There may be some delay between the occurrence of the original events and the processing of data. Compare with real time.

baud /bɔːd/ *n* A unit for measuring the rate of data transmission. One baud = 1 bit per second. Named after Baudot, a pioneer of telegraphic communication.

binary digit /'baɪnərɪ ‚dɪdʒɪt/ *n* The smallest unit of information in the binary system, 0 or 1. Also called bit.

binary system /'baɪnərɪ ‚sɪstəm/ *n* A notation system in which the base for each digital position is 2. In this system numbers are represented by the two digits 0 and 1. Thus the binary number 10 represents 2 in the decimal system, while 100 represents 4.

bit-mapped display /'bɪtmæpt dɪs‚pleɪ/ *n* A display that stores pixel information in RAM memory cells.

bookmark /'bʊkmɑːk/ *n* A saved link that takes users directly to a Web address. Bookmarks are also called hotlist entries or favourites.

boot /buːt/ *v* To start up a computer.

bridge /brɪdʒ/ *n* A device used to connect groups of computers.

browser /'braʊzə(r)/ *n* A program designed to fetch and display Web pages on the Internet.

bug /bʌɡ/ *n* An error in a program.

bulletin board /'bʊlətɪn ‚bɔːd/ *n* An online service that allows users to access and send information to other users quickly and easily. Any users who want to send or read messages dial up with their PC and modem combination to the central bulletin board system (BBS). Once connected they can share information and files using various facilities.

bus /bʌs/ *n* A channel, or highway, which carries signals between units in the CPU.

byte /baɪt/ *n* A unit of information which consists of a fixed number of bits (usually 1 byte = 8 bits). A byte can represent any value from 0 to 255. The sequence of bits in a byte represents an instruction, letter, number or any other character. Compare with kilobyte, megabyte, gigabyte, terabyte.

C

cathode ray tube (CRT) /‚kæθəʊd 'reɪ tjuːb/ *n* The picture tube of the display, which is made of glass and contains a vacuum. In a monochrome monitor, the electron beam scans the screen and turns on or off the pixels that make up the black-and-white image. In a colour monitor, the screen surface is coated with triads of red, green and blue phosphor. Three electron guns energize the phosphor dots, causing them to emit coloured light from which the picture is formed.

cell /sel/ *n* An intersection of a column and a row in a spreadsheet.

central processing unit (CPU) /ˌsentrəl ˈprəʊsesɪŋ ˌjuːnɪt/ *n* The 'brain' of the computer. Its function is to execute programs stored in the main memory by fetching their instructions, examining them and then executing them one after another. Its basic components are the control unit, the arithmetic logic unit and the registers. The CPU of a microcomputer is built into a single microprocessor chip.

channel /ˈtʃænl/ *n* An IRC conversation area. There are thousands of channels on the Internet.

character /ˈkærɪktə(r)/ *n* A symbol available on the keyboard (letter, number or blank space).

chat /tʃæt/ *n* A real-time interactive conversation on the Internet. See Internet relay chat.

chip /tʃɪp/ *n* A tiny piece of silicon containing complex electronic circuits. Chips are used to make the hardware components of a computer.

Chooser /ˈtʃuːzə(r)/ *n* A desk accessory supplied by Apple and used to select the printer you wish to use.

client program /ˌklaɪənt ˈprəʊgræm/ *n* Software running on your PC used to connect and obtain data from a server.

client-server /ˌklaɪənt ˈsɜːvə(r)/ *n* A system in which various client programs all connect to a central server to obtain information or to communicate.

Clipart /ˈklɪpɑːt/ *n* Images shipped with graphics packages.

Clipboard /ˈklɪpbɔːd/ *n* A holding place for text or graphics that you have just cut or copied.

coding /ˈkəʊdɪŋ/ *n* The process of writing instructions for a computer.

colour palette /ˈkʌlə ˌpælɪt/ *n* The collection of colours available in a system. Its size depends on the hardware.

command /kəˈmɑːnd/ *n* An order which the computer can obey. Synonymous with 'instruction'.

communications port /kəˌmjuːnɪˈkeɪʃnz ˌpɔːt/ *n* A socket at the back of your computer for a modem.

compact disk /kəmˈpækt ˌdɪsk/ *n* A storage device which uses optical laser techniques and which provides mass storage capacity.

compatibility /kəmˌpætəˈbɪlɪtɪ/ *n* This is said to exist between two computers if programs can be run on both without any

change; it also refers to those applications that are executed in specific types of computers; these applications are 'compatible' with the computer.

compiler /kəmˈpaɪlə(r)/ *n* A special program that converts a source program (written in a high-level language) into an object program (written in a lower-level language).

compression /kəmˈpreʃn/ *n* The process which makes computer data smaller so the information takes less space and may be transmitted in less time. Compressed files have extensions like .zip, .arj, .sit.

configuration /kənˌfɪgjuˈreɪʃən/ *n* The physical components of a computer system.

control unit (CU) /kənˈtrəʊl ˌjuːnɪt/ *n* A component of the CPU which coordinates all the other parts of the computer system. This unit is also responsible for fetching instructions from the main memory and determining their type.

cookies /ˈkukɪz/ *n* Small files used by Web servers to know if you have visited their site before.

co-processor /kəʊˈprəʊsesə(r)/ *n* A silicon chip which performs precise tasks and mathematical operations very rapidly. Sometimes it is called the 'floating-point unit' or FPU.

cracker /ˈkrækə(r)/ *n* An 'intruder' who breaks into computer systems for fun, to steal information, or to propagate viruses.

crash /kræʃ/ **1** *n* A serious failure which usually requires operator attention before the computer system can be restarted. **2** *v* When a hard disk system fails, it is said to have 'crashed'.

cyberspace /ˈsaɪbəspeɪs/ *n* A term originated by William Gibson in his novel *Neuromancer*, now used to refer to the Internet.

D

data /ˈdeɪtə/ *n* Information to be processed by a computer program. Data processing is the performing of operations on data to obtain information or solutions to a problem.

database /ˈdeɪtəbeɪs/ *n* A file of structured data.

database program /ˈdeɪtəbeɪs ˌprəʊgræm/ *n* An applications program used to store, organize and retrieve a large collection of data. Among other facilities, data can be searched, sorted and updated.

data communication system /ˈdeɪtə kəˌmjuːnɪˈkeɪʃən ˌsɪstəm/ *n* A computer system connected by telecommunications links (for data transmission).

data transfer rate /ˈdeɪtə ˈtrænsfə reit/ *n* The average speed required to transmit data

from a disk system to the main memory. Usually measured in megabits per second.

debug /diːˈbʌg/ *v* To correct program errors or 'bugs'.

debugger /diːˈbʌgə/ *n* A tool which lets the user follow the execution of programs one statement at a time, in order to help find errors in the code.

decryption /diːˈkrɪpʃn/ *n* The process of decoding (deciphering) secret data.

default font /dɪˈfɔːlt ˌfɒnt/ *n* A font used by the system until another font is chosen from the menu.

desk accessory /ˌdesk əkˈsesərɪ/ *n* A mini-application available on the Apple Menu. Examples: Calculator, Clock, Scrapbook.

desktop /ˈdesktɒp/ *n* An area of work – the menu bar and other sections of the screen.

desktop publishing (DTP) /ˈdesktɒp ˈpʌblɪʃɪŋ/ *n* The use of a computer system for all steps of document production, including typing, editing, graphics and printing.

dial up /ˈdaɪəl ʌp/ *v* To connect to a network over phone lines using a modem and a computer.

dialog box /ˈdaɪəlɒg ˌbɒks/ *n* A message box requiring information from the user.

directory /daɪ-, dɪˈrektərɪ/ *n* An alphabetical or chronological list of the contents (files) of a disk. Also known as catalogue.

disk /dɪsk/ *n* A storage device made of flat circular plates with magnetizable surfaces. See floppy, hard and optical disks.

disk drive /ˈdɪsk draɪv/ *n* The electronic mechanism that actually reads what is on a disk. If we are talking about hard disks, the disk and the drive are built into a single unit (hard disk = hard drive). If we are talking about floppies, the disk drive is the slot into which you insert a floppy disk.

dithering /ˈdɪðərɪŋ/ *n* The process of mixing two colours to produce an approximation to another colour. By using this shading technique, the human eye will blend the colours, increasing the apparent number of colours on the screen.

domain name /dəˈmeɪn ˌneɪm/ *n* Internet sites are usually identified by a domain name, which consists of two or more parts separated by dots, e.g. http://www.ibm.com. The part on the left, a subdomain, is the most specific (e.g. ibm, whitehouse). The part on the right, a primary domain, is the most general; this can be a country (e.g. fr for France, es for Spain, it for Italy), or the type of organization (e.g. com for commercial, org for organization, edu for education, or net for network). An IP address (e.g. 194.179.73.2) is translated into a domain name (e.g. sendanet.es) by a Domain Name System.

dot-matrix /dɒt ˌmætrɪks/ *n* A regular pattern of dots; conventionally used to refer to dot-matrix printers which, instead of printing formed characters, print an array of dots. There are two main types of dot-matrix printers: the 9-pin and the 24-pin. The two most important emulations for these printers are Epson and IBM Proprinter.

download /daʊnləʊd/ *v* To transfer a file from one computer to another over the telephone.

E

edit /ˈedɪt/ *v* To make changes and corrections to text and graphics. Well-known editing techniques are: 'select', 'undo', 'copy', 'cut' and 'paste' a portion of text.

electronic mail (e-mail) /ˌelektrɒnɪk ˈmeɪl/ *n* A facility which allows users to exchange messages electronically. Here is a typical e-mail address:

leo@sendanet.es

'leo' is the user name, @ means 'at', 'sendanet' is the Internet service provider, and 'es' means the server is based in España (Spain).

encrypt /ɪnˈkrɪpt/ *v* To encode data so that unauthorized users can't read it.

encryption /ɪnˈkrɪpʃn/ *n* The process of encrypting. Data encryption is important for network security, particularly when sending confidential information such as credit card numbers.

EPS format /ˌiːpiːˈes ˌfɔːmæt/ *n* A file format that stands for 'Encapsulated PostScript'. It stores a file in a form that can be imported into a different file.

execute /ˈeksɪkjuːt/ *v* To perform the operations specified by a routine or instruction. Execute a program: run a program in a computer.

expansion slots /ɪkˈspænʃn slɒts/ *n* The connectors that allow the user to install expansion boards to improve the computer's performance.

F

fault tolerance /fɔːlt ˌtɒlərəns/ *n* A technique to protect data from hardware failures such as disk crashes, bad controllers or the destruction of important information on a file server. Fault-tolerant systems are essential for LAN installations.

fax /fæks/ *n* A facsimile machine that operates by scanning a document so that the image is sent to a receiving machine which produces a copy of the original.

field /fiːld/ *n* A unit of information in a 'record'. In a database, information is entered via fields.

file /faɪl/ *n* **1** A collection of records (in a database). **2** A section of information stored on disk – a document or an application.

file compression /faɪl kəmˈpreʃn/ *n* The encoding of a file into a more compact format so that it occupies less disk space.

file server /faɪl ˈsɜːʌə/ *n* The combination of a software controller and a mass storage device which allows various users to share common files and applications (in a network).

finger /ˈfɪŋgə/ *n* A program that helps you find people on other Internet sites.

firewall /ˈfaɪəwɔːl/ *n* A software and hardware device that allows limited access to an internal network from the Internet. This prevents intruders from stealing or destroying confidential data.

firmware /ˈfɜːmweə/ *n* Permanent software instructions contained in the ROM.

flame /fleɪm/ *n* An angry or insulting comment on a discussion group (on the Internet).

floppy disk /ˌflɒpi ˈdɪsk/ *n* A disk made of a flexible plastic material upon which data is stored on magnetic tracks.

flowchart /ˈfləʊtʃɑːt/ *n* A diagram or symbolic representation which shows the logical steps of a computer program.

flush /flʌʃ/ *adj* A line of type is said to be 'flush' when there is no space between it and a reference line. For example, text that is 'flush left' is aligned with the left margin of a page.

folder /ˈfəʊldə/ *n* A holder of documents, applications and other folders on the Macintosh desktop. Folders (similar to subdirectories in other systems) allow you to organize information in different levels.

font /fɒnt/ *n* The shape, style and size of a particular typeface, e.g. Times Bold at 10pt; **resident font** /ˈrezɪdənt ˌfɒnt/ *n* A font included in a laser printer's memory. (If a font is not resident, the printer has to load it from the computer, which takes up RAM from the printer.)

font formats
– PostScript Type 1 & 2, scalable font formats from Adobe Systems.
– Speedo, scalable font format from Bitstream.
– Truetype, scalable font format from Apple and Microsoft.

format /ˈfɔːmæt/ **1** *n* The layout of a document, including page numbers, line spaces, margins, paragraph alignment, headers and footers, etc. **2 format a disk** *v* To prepare a disk for use. When a disk is initialized, the operating system marks tracks and sectors on its surface.

fragmentation /ˌfrægmenˈteɪʃn/ *n* Disk performance can be affected by fragmentation. When the operating system cannot find enough contiguous space to store a complete file, the file is divided into several separated fragments. As disk fragmentation increases, disk efficiency starts decreasing.

frames /freɪmz/ *n* Subdivided areas of the screen. Some Web sites have frames or separate windows within the main window.

freeware /ˈfriːweə/ *n* Software that is available free of charge for public use.

function key /ˈfʌŋkʃən ˌkiː/ *n* A key on a computer keyboard which causes a specific operation to take place, other than the entry of a standard character. What function keys do depends on the program.

G

gateway /ˈgeɪtweɪ/ *n* A device used to interconnect different types of networks.

gigabyte /ˈgɪgəbaɪt/ *n* 1,024 megabytes.

graphics tablet /ˈgræfɪks ˌtæblɪt/ *n* An input device which allows the user to specify a position on the screen by using a stylus. Tablets are more accurate than other devices.

graphical user information (GUI) /ˈgræfɪkəl ˌjuːzər ˈɪntəfeɪs/ *n* An operating environment based on graphics (windows, icons, pop-up menus), mouse and pointer, e.g. the Macintosh system, Microsoft Windows, IBM OS/2 Warp or OSF Motif.

graphics package /ˈgræfɪks ˌpækɪdʒ/ *n* Software that allows the user to create and run graphics programs.

H

hacker /ˈhækə(r)/ *n* Someone who invades a network's privacy.

hard disk /ˌhɑːd ˈdɪsk/ *n* A disk made from a solid magnetic material used as a storage device. There are different versions: fixed (internal, external), removable, etc. Compare with optical disks.

hardware /ˈhɑːdweə/ *n* The physical units which make up a computer system. See software.

hexadecimal system /ˌheksəˈdesɪməl ˌsɪstəm/ *n* The notation of numbers to the base of 16. The ten decimal digits 0 to 9 are used, and in addition six more digits – A, B, C, D, E and F – to represent 10 to 15.

high-level language /ˌhaɪ ˌlevəl ˈlæŋgwɪdʒ/ *n* A language in which each statement represents several machine code instructions, e.g. FORTRAN, COBOL, LISP, etc.

home page /ˌhəʊm ˈpeɪdʒ/ n **1** The first page of a Web site that contains links to other pages; **2** The default start-up page on which a Web browser starts.

host /həʊst/ n The computer which you contact to access the Internet.

hyperlink /ˈhaɪpəlɪŋk/ n Text, image or button that connects to other destinations on the Web. It is like an embedded Web address that you can click.

hypermedia /ˌhaɪpəˈmiːdɪə/ n A combination of hypertext and multimedia. A hypermedia document integrates different formats (text, graphics, sound, and video) and contains links that take you to other resources.

hypertext /ˈhaɪpətekst/ n Text that contains links to other documents. The codes used to create hypertext documents are called HTML. See also Web.

hyphenation /ˌhaɪfəˈneɪʃən/ n The division of words into syllables by a short dash '-' or hyphen. To produce lines of equal length, word processors hyphenate words instead of stretching word spaces too much.

I

icon /ˈaɪkɒn/ n A small picture representing an object, process or function.

image map /ˈɪmɪdʒ ˌmæp/ n A clickable image that sends you to different Web pages depending on the area you click.

inch /ɪntʃ/ n The equivalent of 2.54 cm, or 72.27 points.

indentation /ˌɪndenˈteɪʃən/ n This moves the edge of the text away from the margins towards the centre of the page.

INITs /ˈɪnɪts/ n System utilities activated when the computer is turned on.

ink-jet printer /ˈɪŋk dʒet ˌprɪntə(r)/ n A printer that generates an image by spraying tiny droplets of ink at the paper. By heating the ink within the print head, individual drops are expelled to make a matrix of dots on the paper.

input /ˈɪnpʊt/ **1** n The process of transferring information into the memory from some peripheral unit. **2** v To transfer data, or program instructions, into the computer.

input devices /ˈɪnpʊt dɪˌvaɪsɪz/ n Units of hardware which allow the user to enter information into the computer, e.g. the keyboard, mouse, trackball, lightpen, graphics tablet, voice recognition devices.

integrated package /ˈɪntəgreɪtɪd ˈpækɪdʒ/ n Software which includes a family of applications – typically spreadsheet, word processor, database and graphics and communications modules. The modules are linked by a common user interface.

interface /ˈɪntəfeɪs/ n Channels and control circuits which provide a connection between the CPU and the peripherals. See also user interface.

internal memory /ɪnˈtɜːnəl ˌmemərɪ/ n See main memory.

Internet /ˈɪntənet/ n A global network of computer networks which facilitates data communication services such as e-mail, file transfer, information retrieval and newsgroups.

Internet relay chat /ˈɪntənet ˈriːleɪ ˈtʃæt/ n A system that allows many people to have live conversations (usually typed) simultaneously on the Internet.

Internet telephone /ˈɪntənet ˈtelɪfəʊn/ n A system that allows people to make phone calls via the Internet.

Internet TV /ˈɪntənet ˈtiː ˈviː/ n A TV set used as an Internet device.

interpreter /ɪnˈtɜːprɪtə/ n A programming environment that executes statements directly, avoiding the need for compilation.

Intranet /ˈɪntrənet/ n An internal company network which uses public Internet software but makes the Web site only accessible to employees and authorized users.

IP address /ˌaɪ ˈpiː əˈdres/ n A number which identifies a computer on the Internet. Every machine on the Internet has a unique IP address, e.g. 194.179.73.2

J

Java /ˈdʒɑːvə/ n The cross-platform programming language from Sun Microsystems for building Internet applications.

joystick /ˈdʒɔɪstɪk/ n An input device with a vertical lever used in computer games to move the cursor around the screen.

justification /ˌdʒʌstɪfɪˈkeɪʃən/ n The process by which the space between the words and letters in a line of type is evenly divided to produce a line that is flush with both left and right margin.

K

kerning /ˈkɜːnɪŋ/ n The process of adjusting the spaces between letters to achieve even, consistent letter spacing.

key pals /ˈkiːpælz/ n Pen pals (pen friends) that exchange e-mail messages.

keyboard /ˈkiːbɔːd/ n An input device with typewriter keys for letters, numbers and line controllers. It may also have function keys for special purposes.

kilobit /ˈkɪləbɪt/ n One thousand bits; unit used to measure the bandwidth of transmission, e.g. 56 kilobits per second.

kilobyte /ˈkɪləbaɪt/ n A unit for measuring the memory or disk space in thousands of bytes. Also called k = 1,024 bytes.

L

laptop /ˈlæptɒp/ n A small type of portable computer.

laser printer /ˈleɪzə ˌprɪntə(r)/ n A non-impact printer that takes in data from the computer and builds up an image of the page in its own internal memory. A laser beam traces the image's dot pattern onto a rotating photosensitive drum, placing a static charge on the exposed areas. As the drum rotates, the toner particles are attracted to the charged areas. Then an electrically-charged wire pulls the toner particles off the drum, and they fall onto the paper.

lightpen /ˈlaɪtpen/ n A highly sensitive photo-electric device which uses the CRT screen as the positioning reference. The user can pass the pen over the surface of the screen to detect, draw or modify images displayed on the screen.

link /lɪŋk/ n See hyperlink.

list server /ˈlɪst ˌsɜːvə(r)/ n See mailing list.

load /ləʊd/ v To read program instructions into the main memory.

local area network (LAN) /ˌləʊkəl ˈeərɪə ˈnetwɜːk (læn)/ n A network contained in a relatively small area.

login /ˈlɒgɪn/ n The act of identifying yourself when entering a network. You usually type your user name and password.

log on /ˌlɒg ˈɒn/ v To connect to a network, FTP site or Telnet remote system.

log off /ˌlɒg ˈɒf/ v To disconnect from a network or online system.

low-level language /ˌləʊ ˌlevəl ˈlæŋgwɪdʒ/ n A language in which each instruction has a corresponding machine code equivalent.

M

machine code /məˈʃiːn kəʊd/ n Binary code numbers, the only language that computers can understand directly.

macro /ˈmækrəʊ/ n **1** An abbreviation for 'macro-instruction'. **2** A stored set of commands, control sequences or definitions that is substituted for the macro name when that name is invoked.

mailing list /ˈmeɪlɪŋ ˌlɪst/ n A system that allows people to send e-mail to one address. The messages are then distributed to all the subscribers. Mailing lists are usually discussion groups which connect people with common interests.

mail merging /ˈmeɪl ˌmɜːdʒɪŋ/ n The process of combining a database file with a word processor to personalize a standard letter.

mainframe /'meɪnfreɪm/ *n* The largest and most powerful type of computers. Mainframes process enormous amounts of data and are used in large installations.

main memory /ˌmeɪn 'meməri/ *n* The section which holds the instructions and data currently being processed; also referred to as the 'immediate access store', 'primary memory' or 'internal memory'. Microcomputers make use of two types of internal memory: RAM and ROM.

megabit /'megəbɪt/ *n* A million binary digits; used to refer to storage devices.

megabyte /'megəbaɪt/ *n* 1,024 kilobytes.

megahertz /'megəhɜːts/ *n* A unit of a million cycles per second used to measure processor speed.

menu bar /'menjuː ˌbaː/ *n* The area at the top of the screen which allows access to the various menus.

microchip /'maɪkrəʊˌtʃɪp/ *n* See chip.

microprocessor /ˌmaɪkrəʊ'prəʊsesə(r)/ *n* A chip, or integrated circuit, that processes the instructions provided by the software.

mnemonic /nɪ'mɒnɪk/ *n* A label or abbreviation used to make words easier to remember.

modem /'məʊdem/ *n* A device attached to a computer and the telephone line allowing access to wide networks. Standard telephone lines carry analogue signals, so the digital signals used by computers must be converted into the correct form by means of a modem.

monitor /'mɒnɪtə(r)/ *n* A CRT device which displays the computer output. Monochrome monitors display one colour at a time, in contrast to colour monitors which can display many different colours at the same time.

mouse /maʊs/ *n* A small input device with a ball underneath that is rolled by the user to specify the position of the cursor or to make choices from the menu.

multimedia /ˌmʌltɪ'miːdɪə/ *n* This refers to the integration of existing technologies of audio, video, animation and telecommunications with computing. Multimedia applications are also known as hypermedia.

multitasking /ˌmʌltɪ'taːskɪŋ/ *n* The execution of several tasks at the same time.

N

netiquette /'netɪket/ *n* Rules of etiquette ('good manners') when sending messages to a mailing list or newsgroup.

network /'netwɜːk/ *n* A system of computer devices (e.g. CPUs, printers) or 'nodes' interconnected so that information and resources can be shared by a large number of users.

newsgroups /'njuːzˌgruːps/ *n* The public discussion areas which make up Usenet.

newsreader /'njuːzˌriːdə/ *n* A program that reads and sends articles to newsgroups.

node /nəʊd/ *n* A point on a junction of communication lines in a network. In a communications network, various computer devices (nodes) are interconnected to permit information to be interchanged between those devices.

O

object language /'ɒbdʒɪkt ˌlæŋgwɪdʒ/ *n* A language or set of instructions into which a source language is translated by a compiler.

object-oriented programming /'ɒbdʒɪkt 'ɔːrientɪd 'prəʊgræmɪŋ/ *n* A programming technique that allows the creation of 'objects' which can be reused, or used as the foundation of others. Used to develop complex programs, especially GUI programs.

octal system /'ɒktəl ˌsɪstəm/ *n* The notation of numbers using 8 as a base or radix.

offline /'ɒf laɪn/ *adj* Not connected to the net.

online /'ɒn laɪn/ *adj* Connected to the net.

operating system /'ɒpəreɪtɪŋ ˌsɪstəm/ *n* The programs and routines which allow a computer to operate; it usually consists of a group of programs which coordinate the software and hardware of a computer system.

optical character recognition /ˌɒptɪkəl 'kærɪktə rekəgˌnɪʃən/ *n* Technology that allows computers to recognize text input into a system with a scanner. After a page has been scanned, an OCR program identifies fonts, styles and graphic areas.

optical disk /ˌɒptɪkəl 'dɪsk/ *n* A storage device in which data is recorded as microscopic 'pits' by a laser beam. The data is read by photoelectric sensors which do not make active contact with the storage medium.

optical fibre cable /ˌɒptɪkəl 'faɪbə ˌkeɪbəl/ *n* A type of cable that guides light impulses at high frequencies along the glass fibre.

output /'aʊtpʊt/ **1** *n* The results produced by a computer. **2** *v* To transfer information from a CPU to an output device.

output devices /'aʊtpʊt dɪˌvaɪsɪz/ *n* The units of hardware which display the results produced by the computer (e.g. plotters, printers, monitors).

P

page description language /ˌpeɪdʒ dɪs'krɪpʃən ˌlæŋgwɪdʒ/ *n* A computer language that describes how to print the text and images on each page of the document.

palmtop /'paːmtɒp/ *n* A hand-held computer which is used as PC companion.

parallel port /'pærəlel 'pɔːt/ *n* An interface port on a printer used to communicate with the computer. It transmits and receives 8 bits of data side by side. Compare with serial port.

Pascal /'pæs'kæl/ A high-level language, named after Blaise Pascal.

password /'paːswɜːd/ *n* A secret word which must be entered before access is given to a computer system.

patterns /'pætənz/ *n* A menu or palette from which the user can pick the required pattern to fill shapes and draw borders.

peripherals /pə'rɪfərəlz/ *n* The units connected to the CPU: input devices, output devices and storage devices.

phosphor /'fɒsfər/ *n* The material or substance of the CRT screen that lights up when struck by an electron beam.

photosetter /'fəʊtəʊˌsetə/ *n* A printer that sets type by a photographic process or on photographic film that allows for high resolution.

pica /'paɪkə/ *n* A unit of 4.23 mm used in typography.

piracy /'paɪərəsi/ *n* The illegal copying of programs.

pixel /'pɪksəl/ *n* The smallest element of a display surface. In monochrome monitors, one pixel is the visual representation of a bit in the refresh buffer (the memory used for storing the picture for screen refresh). The pixel is white if the bit is 0, and black if the bit is 1. In colour monitors, each pixel can represent various bits.

platform /'plætfɔːm/ *n* A type of computer system, e.g. IBM PCs and compatibles, Macintosh computers.

plot /plɒt/ *v* To draw lines connecting the points on a graph.

plotter /'plɒtə(r)/ *n* A very common graphics output device which is used to make various types of engineering drawings.

plug-ins /'plʌgɪnz/ *n* Special programs which extend the capabilities of a browser so that it can handle audio, video, 3-D and animation.

point /pɔɪnt/ *n* A unit used to measure font types and the distance between baselines. A point is a subdivision of a pica: there are 12 points in a pica and 72.27 points in an inch.

pointer /'pɔɪntə(r)/ *n* **1** A small picture that follows the mouse movements. **2** The cursor which locates the insertion point on the screen, i.e. indicates where the next character will be displayed.

port /pɔːt/ *n* A socket or channel in the rear panel of the computer into which you can plug a wide range of peripherals: modems, fax machines, hard drives, etc.

PostScript /ˈpəʊsskrɪpt/ *n* A page description or graphics language developed by Adobe Systems Inc. A PostScript font is any font – such as Times or Helvetica – that is defined in the PostScript language.

primary colours /ˌpraɪmərɪ ˈkʌləz/ *n* These are red, green and blue in computers. Compare with the colours considered basic in inks (magenta, yellow and cyan).

primitives /ˈprɪmɪtɪvz/ *n* The basic shapes used to construct graphical objects: lines, polygons, etc.

printer /ˈprɪntə(r)/ *n* An output device which converts data into printed form. The output from a printer is referred to as a print-out. There are various types of printers: laser, dot-matrix, ink-jet, thermal, etc.

printer driver /ˈprɪntəˌdraɪvə(r)/ *n* A program installed to control a particular type of printer.

program /ˈprəʊgræm/ *n* A set of instructions for solving a specific problem by computer.

programming /ˈprəʊgræmɪŋ/ *n* The process by which a set of instructions is produced for a computer to make it perform a specified task. The task can be anything from the solution to a mathematical problem to the production of a graphics package.

protocol /ˈprəʊtəkɒl/ *n* A set of rules which determine the formats by which information may be exchanged between different systems.

proxy /ˈprɒksɪ/ *n* A special server which controls the traffic between the Internet and a private network. Thanks to this server all the computers of an internal network can access the Internet simultaneously. A proxy also contains security mechanisms. See also firewall.

Q

quit /kwɪt/ *v* To leave a program.

R

random access memory (RAM) /ˌrændəm ˈækses ˌmeməri (ræm)/ *n* The part of the main memory which stores information temporarily while you are working. RAM requires a continuous power supply to retain information. Compare with ROM.

RAM cache *n* A certain amount of RAM memory which can be designated to store information that an application uses repeatedly.

read only memory (ROM) /ˌriːd ˈəʊnlɪ ˌmeməri (rɒm)/ *n* Chips of memory containing information which is present and permanent.

real time /ˈrɪəl ˌtaɪm/ *adj* Involving the processing of data input to a system at almost the same time as the event which generates the data. Compare with batch processing.

reboot /rɪˈbuːt/ *v* To restart the computer.

record /ˈrekɔːd/ *n* A unit of a file consisting of a number of interrelated data elements (fields).

recording heads /rɪˈkɔːdɪŋ ˌhedz/ *n* The read/write heads of disk drives.

refresh rate /rɪˈfreʃ reɪt/ *n* The number of times per second the display screen is scanned, creating the pixels. Also known as the 'scan rate'. (A refresh rate of 70 Hz or more is needed if flicker is to be avoided.)

register /ˈredʒɪstə(r)/ *n* The component in the processor or other chip which holds the instruction from the memory while it is being executed.

resolution /ˌrezəˈluːʃən/ *n* The maximum number of pixels in the horizontal and vertical directions of the screen; also refers to the number of pixels per inch.

router /ˈruːtə(r)/ *n* A device used to connect various LANs.

routine /ruːˈtiːn/ *n* A piece of code which performs a specific function or task in the operation of a program or system.

ruler icons /ˈruːlər ˌaɪkɒnz/ *n* Small graphics representing different format options – tab stops, paragraph alignment, line spacing, etc. – which are displayed in rows at the top of a Windows screen.

S

save /seɪv/ *v* To copy information from the RAM to a disk.

scale /skeɪl/ *v* 1 To magnify or shrink a particular font in order to use it at a range of point sizes. 2 To make an object larger or smaller in any direction.

scanner /ˈskænə(r)/ *n* An input device that scans (reads) the image as a series of dots and introduces the information into the computer's memory. Flatbed scanners have a flat surface. Slide scanners work with 35 mm slides.

Scrapbook /ˈskræpbʊk/ *n* A desk accessory in which you can keep images and text. You can copy, cut and paste frequently used pictures.

screen saver /ˈskriːn seɪvə(r)/ *n* A program that darkens the screen after you have not worked for several minutes. Designed to protect an unchanging image from burning into the screen, but used more often as a status symbol.

scroll /skrəʊl/ *v* To move a document in its window by using scroll bars so that text in another part of the document is visible.

search engine /ˈsɜːtʃ ˌendʒɪn/ *n* A program that allows users to search a large database of Web addresses and Internet resources. Examples of search engines are Yahoo, Altavista, Lycos.

secondary memory /ˌsekəndərɪ ˈmeməri/ *n* See backing store.

sector /ˈsektə(r)/ *n* A part of a track or band of a magnetic disk.

serial port /ˌsɪərɪəl ˈpɔːt/ *n* An interface port on a modem, mouse or printer used to communicate with the computer. It transmits and receives bits of data one after the other. Compare with parallel port.

shareware /ˈʃeəweə/ *n* Programs that are distributed free, via an electronic bulletin board or on a disk from user groups. The programmer usually requests that you send £5 or £10 to him or her, but only if you like the software.

silicon chip /ˈsɪlɪkən tʃɪp/ *n* A device made up of a non-metallic semiconducting material (silicon), which contains a set of integrated circuits, with high-speed performance.

single in-line memory modules (SIMMs) /ˌsɪŋgəl ɪn laɪn ˈmeməri ˌmɒdjuːlz/ *n* Boards containing RAM chips, connected to the mainboard of the computer.

smileys /ˈsmaɪlɪz/ *n* Faces made from punctuation characters to express emotions in e-mail messages.

snail mail /ˈsneɪl ˌmeɪl/ *n* Conventional mail delivered very slowly, in contrast with e-mail.

software /ˈsɒftweə/ *n* Programs or instructions executed by the computer. See hardware.

source program /ˈsɔːs ˌprəʊgræm/ *n* A program written in a source language, i.e. a programming language which cannot be directly processed by the hardware but requires 'compilation' into an 'object program'.

spell checker /ˈspel ˌtʃekə/ *n* A utility to correct typing mistakes. Some programs are able to correct grammar and style.

spooler /ˈspuːlə/ *n* A utility which makes it possible to send one document to the printer (by creating a temporary file for it) so that the user can work on another.

spreadsheet /ˈspredʃiːt/ *n* An application program for financial planning which allows the user to analyse information presented in tabular form, by manipulating rows and columns.

style /staɪl/ *n* A distinguishing visual characteristic of a typeface, e.g. plain text, italic, bold, etc.

subroutine /'sʌbruːtiːn/ *n* A set of instructions which performs a specific function of the program.

T

tags /tægz/ *n* Codes used in an HTML document to mark the start, end or exact location of a formatting feature or a link on a Web page.

teletext /'telɪˌtekst/ *n* A method of communicating information by using TV signals. An extra signal is broadcast with the TV picture and translated into text on the screen by a decoder.

telex /'teleks/ *n* An automatic exchange service which uses telegraphic equipment (e.g. teleprinters).

Telnet /'telnet/ *n* A network program which is used to log directly into remote computer systems. This enables you to run programs kept on them and edit files directly.

terabyte /'terəbaɪt/ *n* 1,024 gigabytes.

terminal /'tɜːmɪnəl/ *n* A visual display unit where data may be input to or output from a data communications system.

thesaurus /θɪ'sɔːrəs/ *n* A utility for searching synonyms and antonyms. Word finder.

three-dimensional (3-D) /ˌθriː-dɪ'menʃənəl/ *adj* 3-D drawings have depth.

token /'təʊkən/ *n* A special unit of data which acts as a key on a Token Ring network; only the adapter in possession of the token can transmit on the network.

track /træk/ *n* An area marked on the surface of a disk. When a disk is initialized, the operating system divides the surface of the disk into circular tracks, each one containing several sectors. A floppy disk usually contains 80 tracks. Tracks and sectors are used to organize the information stored on disk.

trackball /'trækbɔːl/ *n* A stationary device that works like a mouse turned upside down. The ball spins freely to control the movement of the cursor on the screen.

transceiver /træn'ziːvə(r)/ *n* A **trans**mitter and re**ceiver**: a hardware component that sends and receives network signals.

transformation /ˌtrænsfə'meɪʃən/ *n* The manipulation of an object by moving, rotating or scaling it.

two-dimensional (2-D) /ˌtuː-dɪ'menʃənəl/ *adj* 2-D drawings have no depth (they look flat).

typeface /'taɪpfeɪs/ *n* A set of visually related shapes for the characters of a script. A bit-mapped typeface is one where the characters are stored as images made up of dots. A bit-mapped typeface cannot be altered in size. A scalable typeface is one where the outline of the characters is stored with formulae which adjust the outline as the font is enlarged or shrunk.

typeset /'taɪpset/ *v* To set text as type.

U

UNIX /'juːnɪks/ *n* A popular operating system designed by Bell Laboratories in the USA and widely adopted by many manufacturers.

update /ʌp'deɪt/ *v* To correct, add or delete information in a file and thus ensure that the file reflects the latest situation.

upgrade /ʌp'greɪd/ *v* To add or replace hardware or software in order to expand the computer's power.

upload /ˌʌp'ləʊd/ *v* To send a file from one computer to another via a modem.

Usenet /'juːsˌnet/ *n* A large collection of discussion areas (called 'newsgroups') on the Internet.

user-friendly /ˌjuːzə 'frendlɪ/ *adj* An expression used to describe computers which are designed to be easy to use, by means of self-explanatory interaction between users and computer.

user interface /ˌjuːzər 'ɪntəfeɪs/ *n* The standard procedures for interaction with specific computers.

utility /juː'tɪlɪtɪ/ *n* A small program designed to improve the performance of the system. The term 'system utility' refers to a diverse field covering anything from software designed to help you back up your hard disk or locate files, to anti-virus programs or routines used by the system.

V

videotex /'vɪdɪəʊteks/ *n* A viewdata service that uses telephone lines to transmit data and information; it provides services such as tele-banking and tele-shopping.

virtual interface /ˌvɜːtjʊəl 'ɪntəfeɪs/ *n* A type of interface in which the user puts on a set of special goggles as a display, a controlling device (such as a glove) and a motion detector that allows a computer to sense when and how the user moves. What the user sees is an artificial, computer-generated world in which they can move.

virtual reality /ˌvɜːtjʊəl rɪ'ælətɪ/ *n* A computer-generated space in which the user interacts with artificial objects and environments through three-dimensional computer simulation. This is done by using sensory peripherals such as data gloves and head-mounted displays to give the feeling of being immersed into an illusionary, yet sensate, world.

virus /'vaɪərəs/ *n* A piece of software which attaches itself to an application or file. Once you run an infected application, the virus quickly spreads to the system files and other software. Some viruses can delete files or destroy the contents of hard disks.

voxel /'vɒksəl/ *n* A volume element, analogous to pixels. In spatial-partitioning representations, a solid can be decomposed into cubic cells (voxels).

W

Web /web/ *n* A hypertext-based system by which you can navigate through the Internet. By using a special program known as a 'browser' you can find news, pictures, virtual museums, electronic magazines – any topic you can imagine. You travel through the Web pages by clicking on keywords that take you to other pages or other Web sites. It is also known as the World Wide Web or WWW.

Web site /'web saɪt/ *n* A location on the Internet where a company puts Web pages with information.

wide area network (WAN) /ˌwaɪd ˌeərɪə 'netwɜːk (wæn)/ *n* A network that extends outside a building or small area. For long-distance communications, LANs are usually connected into a WAN.

widow /'wɪdəʊ/ *n* A single line ending a paragraph and appearing at the top of a printed page or column.

window /'wɪndəʊ/ *n* A rectangle on the desktop that displays information.

window-based /'wɪndəʊ ˌbeɪst/ *adj* This refers to an application or program whose interface is based around windows.

word processor /'wɜːd ˌprəʊsesə(r)/ *n* An application that manipulates text and produces documents suitable for printing.

word wrap /'wɜːd ˌræp/ *n* An editing facility which automatically moves a word to the next line if there is not enough space for the complete word on the current line.

workstation /'wɜːksteɪʃən/ *n* A computer system which usually includes a defined collection of input and output devices.

Acronyms and abbreviations

ACK positive ACKnowledgement
ADB Apple Desktop Bus
ADC Analogue to Digital Converter
AI Artificial Intelligence
AIFF Audio Image File Format
ALGOL ALGOrithmic Language, a problem-oriented, high-level programming language for mathematical and scientific use
ALU Arithmetic Logic Unit
AMD Advanced Micro Devices, manufacturer of microprocessors
API Application Program Interface
ASCII American Standard Code for Information Interchange
AT Advanced Technology. The AT was born in 1984 with the introduction of the IBM PC-AT. Most ATs have 286 processors
AT&T American Telephone & Telegraph company
ATM 1 Adobe Type Manager **2** Automated Telling Machine
AVI Audio Video Interface, a video format

BASIC Beginner's All-purpose Symbolic Instruction Code
Bcc Blind carbon copy. Addresses in the Bcc: line of an e-mail will receive a copy of the message but the identity of the recipients will be kept secret
BBS Bulletin Board System
BCPL system programming language from which the language *C* was derived
BIOS Basic Input/Output System
bit binary digit
bps bits per second
BUS Binary Unit System

C A high-level language designed for system programming, usually (but not exclusively) for software development in the UNIX environment
CAD Computer-Aided Design
CAE Computer-Aided Engineering
CAI Computer-Assisted Instruction
CALL Computer-Assisted Language Learning
CAM Computer-Aided Manufacturing
CASE Computer-Aided Software Engineering
Cc Carbon copy. Addresses on the Cc: line of an e-mail will receive the same message.
CD Compact Disk
CD-R Compact Disk-Recordable
CD-ROM Compact Disk-Read Only Memory

CD-RW CD-Rewritable
CGA Colour Graphics Adaptor
CMYB Cyan, Magenta, Yellow, Black
COBOL COmmon Business-Oriented Language
COM Computer Output on Microfilm
cps 1 characters per second **2** cycles per second
CPU Central Processing Unit
CR Carriage Return
CRT Cathode Ray Tube
CU Control Unit

DA Desk Accessory
DAC Digital to Analogue Converter
DAT Digital Audiotape. DAT decks are becoming the standard for professional music recording
DBMS DataBase Management System
DD 1 Disk Drive **2** Double Density
DDE Dynamic Data Exchange
DEC Digital Equipment Corporation
DNS Domain Name System
DOS Disk Operating System
dpi dots per inch
DRAW Direct Read After Write
DR DOS Digital Research disk operating system
DS disks double sided disks
DTP Desktop Publishing
DTV Desktop Video
DVD Digital Video Disk (or Digital Versatile Disk)
DVI Device Independent

EAROM Electrically Alterable Read-Only Memory
ECMA European Computer Manufacturers' Association
EDIF Electronic Data Interchange Format
EGA Enhanced Graphics Adaptor
EOD Erasable Optical Disk
EPRAM Erasable Programmable RAM
EPS(F) Encapsulated PostScript (file)

FAQ Frequently Asked Questions, a file containing answers to questions that the Internet users frequently ask
FD Floppy Disk
FDD Floppy Disk Drive
FDDI Fibre Distributed Data Interface
FDHD Floppy Disk High Density
FORTRAN FORmula TRANslation
FPU Floating-point Unit
FTP File Transfer Protocol

GB Gigabyte (1,024 megabytes)

GCR Group-Coded Recording (format to recognize disks, Macintosh)
GHz Gigahertz: one billion cycles per second
GIF Graphic Interchange Format
GNU Gnu's Not UNIX
GUI Graphical User Interface
HD 1 Hard Disk **2** High Density disk
HDD Hard Disk Drive
HDTV High-definition Television
HP Hewlett-Packard
HTML Hypertext Markup Language, codes used on the Web pages
HTTP Hypertext Transfer Protocol, the method by which Web pages are transferred from an Internet site to your PC
Hz Hertz (unit of frequency equal to one cycle per second), named after Heinrich Hertz

IAC Inter-application Communications
IBM International Business Machines
IC 1 Interface Converter (Card) **2** Integrated Circuit
ICR Intelligent Character Recognition
IDE Integrated Drive Electronics: a standard hard disk controller
IGES Internal Graphics Exchange Specification
i/f interface
I/O Input/Output
IP Internet Protocol
IRC Internet Relay Chat
ISA Industry Standard Architecture. An ISA bus is 16 bits wide
ISDN Integrated Services Digital Network
ISO International Standard Organization
ISP Internet Service Provider
IT Information Technology

JPEG Joint Photographic Experts' Group: standard in image compression

k 1 kilo, used to denote a thousand **2** 1,024 bytes
KB kilobyte (1,024 bytes)
Kbps kilobits per second
kHz kilohertz: 1,000 cycles per second

LAN Local Area Network
Laser Light Amplification by Stimulated Emission of Radiation
LCD Liquid-Crystal Display
LIMDOW Light Intensity Modulation/Direct Overwrite, a method that allows you to overwrite data on optical disks
LISP LISt Processing: high-level language used for artificial intelligence research

LP Linear Programming

LQ Letter Quality

MB 1 megabyte: one million bytes
 2 Mother Board

MBPS MegaBits Per Second

MC Memory Card

MCA Micro Channel Architecture: standard 32-bit bus

MDA Monochrome Display Adaptor

MFM Modified Frequency Modulation (format to recognize disks: IBM and compatibles)

MHz megahertz: one million cycles per second

MIDI Musical Instrument Digital Interface

MIME Multipurpose Internet Mail Extensions, a standard for attaching files to e-mail messages

MIPS Million Instructions Per Second

MMX Multimedia Extensions

modem MOdulator/DEModulator

MP3 MPEG-1 Layer 3 Audio

MPEG Moving Pictures Experts' Group: standard for compressing and decompressing images

ms millisecond: thousandth of a second

MS-DOS Microsoft Disk Operating System

MTBF Mean Time Between Failure. Refers to the average rate of hours for a hard disk

NAK Negative ACKnowledgement

NAS Network Application Support

NIC Network Interface Card

NLQ Near Letter Quality

NUI Network User Identifier

OCR Optical Character Recognition

OLE Microsoft's Object Linking and Embedding standard

OOP Object Oriented Programming

OROM Optical Read Only Memory

OS Operating System

OSF Open Software Foundation

OSI Open System Interconnection

PC Personal Computer

PCI Peripheral Component Interconnect, a standard bus

pdf Portable document formatted to distribute text files over the Internet; it can be read with Adobe Acrobat

PDS Processor Direct Slot

PERT Project Evaluation and Review Technique

PGA Professional Graphics Adaptor

picon picture icon

pixel picture element

PHIGS Programmer's Hierarchical Graphics Interactive Standard

PL/1 Programming Language 1

PMMU Paged Memory Management Unit

PPD PostScript Page Description

ppi pixels per inch

POP Point of Presence, the location you dial into when you want access to the Internet

PPP Point to Point Protocol, allows computers to use modems and to have access to the Internet

PROM Programmable Read Only Memory

PS PostScript

RAM Random Access Memory

RGB Red, Green, Blue

RIP Raster Image Processor

RISC Reduced Instruction Set Computer

ROM Read Only Memory

RS series Requirement Specification, referring to the interconnection standards for computing devices: RS232, RS422 and RS423

SCSI Small Computer System Interface

SIMMs Single In-line Memory Modules: circuit boards which contain RAM chips

SMTP Simple Mail Transfer Protocol

SNA System Network Architecture: data network protocol developed by IBM

TB terabyte: one million megabytes

TCP/IP Transmission Control Protocol/Internet Protocol, the language used for data transfer on the Internet

TELEX TELeprinter EXchange

TIFF Tagged Image File Format: the kind of graphics-file format created by a scanner

TFT Thin Film Transistor: In a TFT display, each pixel is produced by three tiny transistors: one each for red, green and blue. This allows for very clear and stable pictures

TOS Tramiel Operating System

URL Uniform Resource Locator, an address of a Web site's location on the Internet

USB Universal Serial Bus

VAT Value Added Tax

VAX Virtual Address eXtension

VDT Video Display Terminal

VDU Visual Display Unit

VGA Video Graphics Array

VMS Virtual Memory System

VRAM Video Random Access Memory, a common type of video card memory for colourful graphics

VRML Virtual Reality Modelling Language

WAN Wide Area Network

WFW Windows for Workgroups

WIMP Window, Icon, Mouse and Pointer

WORM Write Once/Read Many

WP Word Processor

WWW World Wide Web

WYSIWYG What You See Is What You Get

XGA eXtended Graphics Array

XT eXtended Technology. The XT was born in 1983 with the launch of the IBM PC-XT

Trademarks

We have made every effort to supply trademark information about brand names and products mentioned in this book.

The following are registered trademarks® or trademarks™ of Adobe Systems, Inc.: PostScript, Adobe Type Manager (ATM), Adobe Illustrator, Adobe Photoshop, PageMaker, SuperPaint, Acrobat Reader.

The following are registered trademarks® or trademarks™ of Apple Computer, Inc.: Apple Macintosh, iMac, Power Macintosh, LocalTalk, QuickTime, TrueType, AppleTalk.

The following are registered trademarks® or trademarks™ of Digital Equipment Corporation: DEC, DECtalk, Alpha AXP, MicroVAX, OpenVMS, VAX.

The following are registered trademarks® or trademarks™ of Hewlett-Packard Company: HP, Hewlett-Packard, LaserJet, Vectra.

The following are registered trademarks® or trademarks™ of Intel Corporation: Intel, 286, 386, 486, Pentium, Pentium II, Pentium III.

The following are registered trademarks® or trademarks™ of International Business Machines Corporation: IBM, PC XT, AT, IBM PS/2, PowerPC, Token Ring, OS/2 Warp, VGA, RISC, IBM Proprinter, Aptiva.

The following are registered trademarks® or trademarks™ of International Typeface Corporation: Zapf Chancery, Zapf Dingbats, Bookman, Symbol.

The following are registered trademarks® of Iomega: Jaz, Zip.

The following are registered trademarks® or trademarks™ of Linotype-Hell AG: Linotronic, Courier, Helvetica, Palatino.

The following are registered trademarks® or trademarks™ of Lotus Development Corp. AmiPro, Freelance Graphics, Lotus 1-2-3.

The following are registered trademarks® or trademarks™ of Microsoft Corporation: Cinemania, Microsoft, MS-DOS, MS Word, MS Excel, Windows NT, Windows CE, Windows 2000, PowerPoint, MS Works, MS Access, Windows '95, Windows '98, Internet Explorer, Front Page.

The following are registered trademarks® or trademarks™ of Motorola, Inc.: Motorola 68040, PowerPC.

The following are registered trademarks® or trademarks™ of Sun Microsystems, Inc.: Sun, SuperSPARC, Java.

AMD and K-6 are trademarks of Advanced Micro Devices, Inc.

Arkenstone Open Book Unbound is a trademark of Arkentstone.

AT&T is a trademark of American Telephone & Telegraph Global Information Solutions.

Canvas is a trademark of Deneba Systems.

Compaq Armada is a trademark of Compaq Computer Corp.

CorelDraw and WordPerfect are trademarks of Corel Systems Corp.

Epson and Epson Stylus are trademarks of Epson Ltd.

Ethernet is a registered trademark of Xerox Corporation.

Eudora is a trademark of Qualcomm Incorporated.

Juliet printer is a trademark of Enabling Technologies.

Linux is a trademark of Linus Torvalds.

Macromedia Freehand is a trademark of Macromedia Inc.

mIRC for Windows is a shareware program made by Khaled Mardem-Bey.

*Mobile*Access is a trademark of Mitsubishi.

Motif is a trademark of Open Software Foundation, Inc.

Multimedia Explorer is a trademark of Autodesk.

Netscape Communicator is a trademark of Netscape Communications Corp.

Palm OS is a trademark of 3Com's Palm Computing.

PhotoCD is a trademark of Kodak.

Polywell is a trademark of Polywell, Inc.

Psion is a trademark of Psion PLC.

QuarkXPress is a trademark of Quark, Inc.

Reading Edge OCR is a trademark of Xerox Imaging Systems.

RealAudio is a trademark of RealNetworks, Inc.

Speedo is a tradesmark of Bitstream.

Toshiba is a trademark of Toshiba Corp.

UNIX is a trademark of UNIX System Laboratories, Inc.

Ventura Publisher is a trademark of Ventura Software.

VertPro is a trademark of TeleSensory.

Window Bridge is a trademark of SynthaVoice.

WordStar is a trademark of MicroPro International Corp.

Trademarks are the property of their respective companies.